TWO PATHS TO RICO

*Homesteading, the Great Depression
and Two Journeys to a Small Colorado Mining Town*

TWO PATHS TO RICO

*Homesteading, the Great Depression
and Two Journeys to a Small Colorado Mining Town*

DUANE KEOWN

SUNSTONE
PRESS

SANTA FE

Sunstone books may be purchased for educational, business, or sales promotional use.
For information please write: Special Markets Department, Sunstone Press,
P.O. Box 2321, Santa Fe, New Mexico 87504-2321.

Book and cover design › R. Ahl
Printed on acid-free paper
∞

———————————————

Library of Congress Cataloging-in-Publication Data

Names: Keown, Duane, author.
Title: Two paths to Rico : homesteading, the great depression and two
    journeys to a small Colorado mining town / Duane Keown.
Description: Santa Fe : Sunstone Press, [2021] | Summary: "In the early
    twentieth century two families, one from central Kansas and the other
    from a Missouri cotton farm, left their homes for difficult homestanding
    lives in Dolores County of southwestern Colorado"-- Provided by
    publisher.
Identifiers: LCCN 2021021150 | ISBN 9781632933232 (paperback) | ISBN
    9781632933287 (epub)
Subjects: LCSH: Frontier and pioneer life--Colorado. |
    Depressions--1929--Colorado. | Colorado--History.
Classification: LCC F781 .K46 2021 | DDC 978.8/033--dc23
LC record available at https://lccn.loc.gov/2021021150

———————————————

WWW.SUNSTONEPRESS.COM
SUNSTONE PRESS / POST OFFICE BOX 2321 / SANTA FE, NM 87504-2321 /USA
(505) 988-4418 / FAX (505) 988-1025

CONTENTS

INTRODUCTION

At the Gage farm, two generations: left to right, John Gage, Thomas Keown, Effie Gage, Mary Keown, Herald Keown and Bernice (Gage) Keown.

O h, the regret when you need details to go with a story told by your mother or father about memories important to their lives and backgrounds. Such is the case as I begin this recounting of the journeys of my parents who lived in Rico, Colorado when and where I was born, June 22, 1937. My older sister, Barbara, now deceased, was born at the Johnson Hospital in Cortez. Cortez was on a mostly dirt and partly gravel road fifty miles south of Rico. My younger sister, Beverly, was born in the office of the Rico Argentine Mining Company town doctor, Dr. Sprecher. It doubled as his home.

We don't learn of our parents' past by sitting down to read a book about their histories, but the histories come to us in bits and pieces while growing up.

The old trunk was a rich deposit of Keown and Gage memories. Here is the author and his sister Beverly as they begin to look to the past. (Photograph by Joy Keown)

Herald Keown, my dad, was a storyteller and events along his path to Rico, that I now relate, are only highlights, the high-interest accounts of events significant to him. Many were of hardship in living his teenage years in the experimental town of Blanca, Colorado, where most residents arrived at the same time and lived in tents waiting for the great drawing for parcels of land. The drawing occurred on August 8, 1908. The great town and land development never happened and those who remained tried to endure. His mother baked bread and pies that she sold to the remaining few. In Blanca, Dad and his brother, Urban, developed a passion for playing baseball. Dad was the center fielder for the town team at age fifteen. He played on a team in every community where he lived long enough for the baseball team and fans to become aware of how he could hit the ball. At forty-one, he gave up playing for teams, but his interest never diminished. And it carried over to this author.

From the failed town of Blanca, my granddad filed for a homestead west of Dove Creek, Colorado. Again, with hope of a new beginning, his family built a home and began to farm. It was dry land farming and they depended on rains. Their crop was field corn. But farming didn't make the family of four a living, so my dad went to the mines and mills of Rico and Telluride to support his aging mom, father, and younger brother, who was thirteen when they arrived at Dove Creek. April 6, 1917 the U.S. joined World War I and soon after, Dad, the oldest son of that patriotic family joined the Navy. By then he had a homestead adjoining his father's.

Memories he related to us were mostly in the first four decades of the twentieth century and some may seem improbable as they contrast with our twenty-first century lifestyles and resources. But without a doubt to me, they are true. That is because I heard his best stories many times and I almost knew the next sentence. Each time told there was little alteration. Maybe even a better reason to know they were true stories was that he cherished his reputation for honesty. As the Dolores County Treasurer, and later, Secretary and Treasurer for the Montezuma Valley Irrigation Company, his honesty and exceptional memory served him well. Some of his experiences were so well known to the Montezuma Valley public—farmers paid irrigation water bills at his office—that before he died in 1983, the Cortez Public Librarian and Tom Johnson, a local newspaper reporter, asked him to record on tape his best memories as a pioneer in adjoining Dolores County.

My dad's occupations in meeting the public gave him the opportunity and enjoyment to relate accounts in his long and colorful history. He knew they would grab the taxpayer or water-shareholder's interest, be worthy of time sacrificed for the telling, and even soften the burden of paying taxes or the irrigation water bills. As Treasurer in Rico, many taxpayers would travel up the Dolores River Road, many miles over scenic, but dirt and mountainous roads to Rico to pay their property taxes, but also to visit with my dad. He was more than the County Treasurer. He was a friend and the county's well-known baseball star.

Without many details to the stories told, I remember the highlights of those most captivating. And with some research at county courthouses, town records, libraries, museums, historical societies, and relatives' remembrances, I will recount his and my mom's histories. They are mostly about hardships and misfortunes, but they are also about treasured events they would glory for me to retell and publish.

My mother, Bernice (Gage) Keown's path to the marriage and our Rico home was perhaps with greater privations, worries, and sacrifices than her husband's. Her experiences may have called for even greater endurance and resourcefulness.

From Thayer, Missouri, forced to relocate by her younger brother's illness, the family left their green Missouri cotton farm for the dry climate of Dove Creek. Their family's youngest son, Fay, had complications from rheumatic fever. A much dryer climate for Fay was the Oregon County Missouri doctor's recommendation to prevent an early death. Fay was eight years old, my mother was twelve, and there were four more children: Lura, Edith, Albia and Bryan.

In the bed of an old pre-1920 flatbed truck with sideboards, poor tires, a topless cab, and their belongings on board, they left Thayer in October of 1923. Their destination was a farm they had traded for, part of a homestead, at a site sixteen miles west of Dove Creek. The trade was for a farm unseen at a location called Bug Point. Not only arid, it was also desolate.

The town of Dove Creek in 1923 was only a grocery and mercantile store, a small log cabin and a community get-together building called the Opera House. They camped along the way and rode in the old truck the 1,200 miles to Dove Creek. Unimaginable today, it took more than two weeks. It was Halloween, 1923, the day they arrived and moved into the only house at Bug Point. They began preparation for the winter. The farming season had been over for several months. The nearest school was the Big Valley School, several miles away, so the old truck was transportation to school. Water for the Bug Point home was hauled in barrels from Dove Creek, 25 cents per barrel.

The family wasn't long at Bug Point. The next planting season they moved to an abandoned homestead and took over required improvements to claim the land with a deed.

For mother's older brother Bryan, schooling ended in Missouri. He was eighteen. For mom's brothers Fay and Albia, schooling ended at the eighth grade at the Dove Creek School. Two years were added to the Dove Creek School and mother entered Cortez High School, the nearest high school, as a junior. She boarded with two families and she completed high school in 1929. My aunt Edith's schooling after Dove Creek remains a mystery. Her oldest son, Vernon, says for years he had her diploma from Cortez High School, and he gave it to the youngest brother, Wayne. The diploma was dated 1925 when she would have been eighteen.

From high school in Cortez, Mom with her sister Lura went to Fort

Lewis College near Durango for one year. In those days one year of college qualified for teaching elementary schools. Rural teaching jobs were available; especially where schools were isolated and school boards could barely scrape up the money to pay a teacher. Without a degree my mother taught in three one-room schools in the Dove Creek area. First was the Peel School about ten miles from Dove Creek. The school year began with twenty students in six grades. Then came the Great Depression and an influx of Dust Bowl refugees. Before spring she had fifty-four students, grades one through eight, ages six through sixteen. She was also the janitor and after sweeping the dried mud into a pile and shoveling it out the front door, she walked two miles to where she roomed and boarded with the family of the school board president, who was illiterate. The room where she slept had been tacked on to the house and there were cracks in the walls. She woke early and was often cold. After breakfast with the family, it was all to do over again. She began the long walk to the school. Teacher associations today ask for classes of twenty students in a single grade and teachers are not the janitors.

Mother was not a storyteller, but through her brothers and sisters, my cousins, and especially my dad, I learned of her challenges and the respect her perseverance brought her. She was teaching in the one-room school at the Fairview School in Yellow Jacket, Colorado, twenty miles east of Dove Creek, when she married Dad, on December 1, 1934.

We begin my memories at the Rico baseball field in 1947, when I was eleven.

1

BROKE AT ASHTON AND NEW BEGINNINGS AT BLANCA

The flat spot for everything that needs a field for play at Rico, Colorado. During the glory years of baseball, it was truly a "field of dreams" for celebrated community teams. Even the smallest communities had a team and for Sunday afternoons it was the entertainment. In 1947 World II vets were home and there was an abundance of players. The Rico field had a grandstand that may have held five hundred fans. Today, on the 4th of July, the Old Timers Picnic is held there. (Photograph by Joy Keown)

Almost two miles from Rico, Colorado the baseball field was the only flat place in the town's region for a baseball game. The Dolores River Canyon is narrow where it runs through Rico and everyone lives on the sides of the canyon. The elevation of Rico is 9,000 feet. That July day in 1947 cars were parked for at least a quarter of a mile north and south along Highway 145 that runs along the east side of the baseball field. Near the bleachers, behind the backstop, cars were parked among the aspen trees. The grandstand was full. The Cortez Veterans of Foreign Wars baseball team—Cortez had two teams—was playing the Rico Miners.

I had turned eleven years old the month before and already was a baseball fan. My dad's passion for the sport had rubbed off. Our family lived in Cortez, but it was only three years before that we left Rico where my dad had been the Dolores County Treasurer. Until 1946, when the county seat went to Dove Creek, and since 1881 when Dolores County was established, Rico had been the county seat. It was a minerals town and the population fluctuated with the need or price of gold, silver, lead, and zinc. I knew my dad had played for the Rico Miners, but Rico wasn't even a quarter the size of Cortez in 1947. It had been much larger during World Wars I and II when strategic minerals were in great demand.

It was the ninth inning. Cortez was ahead and their pitcher had controlled the Rico bats. But Rico was still in the game and their last bat and hope was coming up when a middle-aged man in a Rico uniform, gray and trimmed in purple, began making his way through the people in the grandstand. It was the Rico team manager and he was headed to where my dad and I were sitting. When he got close to us he said where all could hear, "Herald, will you pinch hit?" My dad called him by name and said, "You know I haven't played for more than ten years. I would probably disappoint you and embarrass myself." He turned the manager down. The manager had been a player for the Rico Miners with my dad.

Rico lost but as we drove the dusty dirt and gravel road the 50 miles back to Cortez the whole way back I was wondering about my father's baseball playing days. That Rico manager thought he could hit the Cortez pitcher. Dad had turned fifty-one about a month before that game and it seemed to me he was older than the players on the teams. He was a World War I veteran, too old for World War II. Most of the young players for the Rico and Cortez teams had come home from World War II.

But I was so proud. The manager wanting Dad to pinch hit let me know that he was his honest self when I heard him say a few times, "I could hit the ball."

June 13, 1896, Herald Keown was born in Ashton, Kansas, a farming community west of Arkansas City, Kansas. Today it isn't even an incorporated town. His father, Thomas Keown, owned a home, grocery, and mercantile store, along with a wheat farm. He was also able to loan money.

By 1906, my granddad's family lost nearly everything they owned. It was his debts to banks and the unpaid debts, personal to him and to his businesses. And my dad said that another reason was that Granddad had "too many irons in the fire" and couldn't care for his properties. But his pride kept him from taking bankruptcy. He said they were "honest debts to the banks and he would do his best to pay them," according to Dad. Before Granddad went under financially, he sold 200 acres of their farm and paid the banks what he owed them.

Granddad Thomas Keown about the time he married my Grandmother Mary. (Photograph from the trunk)

The family moved to Arkansas City from Ashton and rented a large home where they kept boarders. Grandmother Mary took care of the home and boarder business, and Grandpa Keown took what jobs he could find. Some of the boarders became Dad's friends and were baseball players for the Arkansas City semipro team. My father, who had not yet become a teenager, probably idealized them. At that early age he caught baseball fever.

While at the Arkansas City home, a well-dressed fellow came by offering land lottery tickets for a new Colorado community to be called Blanca. It would be established in the eastern region of the San Luis Valley of Colorado. Granddad was away on business, and Grandma listened to the salesman and paid him $150 for a land lottery ticket. For the times, it was a very brave venture for the wife to make such a forecast of the family future, especially when they were poor. She waited for her husband's return, anxious to know how he might receive the news. But when my grandfather Thomas returned and heard of the purchase, he said it was time for a change and he liked her investment. In July 1908, they loaded their belongings on the train and were off to Fort Garland, Colorado, which was the nearest town to where Blanca would be.

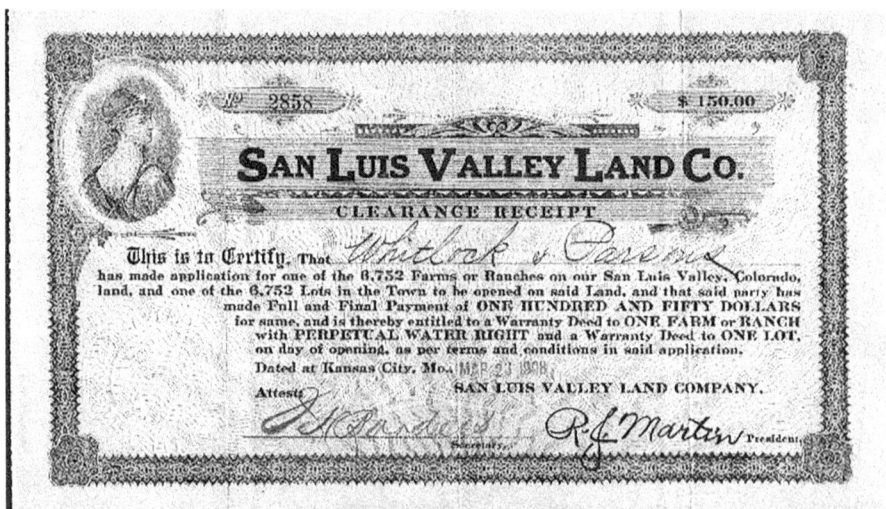

Photograph of a land drawing ticket. It cost $150 and entitled the owner to a lot in the new town of Blanca, a five-acre farm and perpetual water rights. The big prize for the lucky ticket holder at the lottery was a section of land (640 acres is a square mile). There were smaller prizes: two 320 acres tracts, a 120-acre parcel, an 80-acre portion, 20-acre, and ten-acre tracts. (From Blanca Colorado History Page, by Jean Butler)

Streets were laid out where the new town of Blanca was to be located and Dad said theirs was the fourth tent set up. He said before the drawing, tents accommodating 500 persons were at the town site. There were more than 4,000 people at the grand lottery on August 8, 1908. They came in special trains and many by wagons, mainly from the east through Pueblo and Walsenburg, Colorado. Owners of tickets were from all over the country, but especially the Midwest. More than 6,000 tickets were sold.

Blanca would be a new start, especially for Granddad, who was a man of many sorrows. They would be leaving the Arkansas City region where he had so many reminders of his disappointments. My sister, Beverly, says that for many years Grandpa carried a booklet that listed the persons and the amount owed him by his defaulters. He assumed honesty and if the debtors got "on their feet," he would be paid. In an old trunk of World War I vintage that belonged to my father, and now with my sister, we found a rich history of both the Keowns and the Gages. We even found the original list of debts to T.D. Keown that he acquired during the Ashton time. It was in the leather pouch he kept for so many years, hoping honesty would prevail and his debtors would come forward. It even had the IOUs and notarized signatures of the debtors taken at banks in the Ashton and Arkansas City area.

The upper half of the list of T.D. Keown's debtors that he kept until his death in 1937, still hoping the loans would be paid. He even returned from Blanca to the Arkansas City area to collect, but with little success. One dollar in 1900 had the equivalent purchasing power of $28.57 in 2016. Our calculation shows that he was owed $40,283 in today's dollars.

List of notes payable to the order of T. D. Keown.

Amount	Date	Endorsers		Maturity
$12.50	8/5/02	M. L. Phillips L. C.	Geuda Spgs.	8/5/03
	13/5/02	Jas. L. Trotter	Ashton	9 mo.
$43.00	10/1/02	. Y. Willis		10/1/03
36.00	10/17/02	E. P. Tickel I. F. Tickel	Lilivale, Okla	10/17/02
15.76	12/11/02	J. A. Kinzer	Geuda Spgs.	6/11/03
52.75	12/26/02	J. C. Russell,	Ashton, Kan.	6/26/03
45.00	11/21/02	W. B. Fair	Wilbur, Okla.	9/1/03
20.00	11/21/02	W. B. Fair	" "	7/1/03
30.00	11/21/02	W. B. Fair	" "	2/1/03
150.00	10/7/02	Wm. L. Trotter	Ashton, Kan.	10/7/06
32.50	9/9/01	M. P. Hollingsworth	Lilivale, Okla. 1 year	
80.00	9/30/02	B. J. Stockton J. D. Stockton	Geuda Spgs.	9/30/03
29.75	12/17/01	J. H. Fudge	Braman, O. T.	7/1/01
24.70	2/10/03	F. Watson T. Watson		/8/03
80.00	9/29/02	J. G. Osbourn A. le O. C.	Geuda Spgs.	one year
25.00	8/20/02	" " " "	"	8/20/03
50.00	9/17/03	I. N. Carson	Ashton, Kan.	9/17/03
45.00	9/17/02	R. E. Pickett	" "	9/17/03
45.00	8/7/02	J. C. Fair,	Wilbur, Okla.	5/7/02
19.00	9/3/02	W. H. Fair,	Ashton, Kan.	9/3/03
30.00	9/18/02	Willard Wentworth " "		9/13/03
50.00	9/18/01	C. A. Huh,	Portland, "	12 mo.
36.00	3/5/01	Del Prather,	Argonia, "	12/1/02
74.32	1/26/02	J. M. Lee	Ashton, Kan.	9/1/02
40.00	1/6/01	L. A. Palmer	Wilbur, Okla.	9/1/01
70.00	4/8/01	J. J. Wentworth, Ashton, Kan.		17 mo.
141.07	2/7/03	O. W. Cowman,	" "	9 mo.
37.93	2/10/03	Jno. A. Dungan Maria M.	" "	2/10/03

17

The failed businesses of Ashton were not new disappointments to Granddad Keown. In Arkansas City, Grandpa's first wife died in childbirth. Their daughter, Sarah, died young of diphtheria. And his young son, Prowder, by his first wife died at eight years. His second wife, my dad's mother Mary, was fifteen years younger. She was physically strong and was of thriving spirit and character, as the photograph below seems to express.

Grandmother Mary Keown at age twenty-two. (Photograph from the trunk)

With my Grandmother Mary, the Thomas Keowns had three sons. My dad was the oldest; the next born, Berlin, died in infancy in 1900, and the youngest, Urban, was born in 1902.

The old photograph is of Herald Keown at age four. His brother Berlin (in the chair) died in infancy. (Photograph from the trunk)

An old scratched photograph of the Ashton School students is from the trunk. Herald Keown is the last child at the right end of the second row. He was seven and in the first grade at the time of the photograph. (Photograph from the trunk)

Grandma Keown's personality was probably a good match and compensated for her husband's willingness to idealize human character for more than it was. The bold decision to buy the Blanca land drawing ticket was not out of character for her.

But first, about the San Luis Valley and the location of the new town of Blanca that was to be the Keown's new home. The San Luis Valley really isn't a valley as we picture a valley. It is a dry ancient lakebed that we today know as Lake Alamosa. Its beginning was when three to four million years ago volcanoes spread lava and rocks to the south of the valley in the Taos, New Mexico area. The volcanism and its lava and rock stopped the drainage of the Rio Grande River from the San Juan Mountains to the northwest, the Sangre de Cristo Mountains to the northeast, and smaller drainages to the northwest and southeast. Lake Alamosa began to fill until it stretched from near Poncha Pass at the north shore to south of the towns of Antonito and San Luis. The lake may have been 200 feet deep. But contrary to common belief, Lake Alamosa did not empty at the end of the last Ice Age, 11,000 years ago. It emptied about 440 thousand years ago during an interglacial time in the Pleistocene, known commonly as the Ice Age.

During interglacial times the earth's temperature rose and mountains surrounding the lake's glacial runoff raised the water level of Lake Alamosa. At the southeast end of the lake, runoff began to cut through the rock and lava. Relatively soon, the runoff from Lake Alamosa carved through the basalt rock of the volcanic eruptions from three to four million years prior. When the lake emptied, it left a lakebed that is approximately 8,000 square miles and its average elevation is 7,664 feet. It is 122 miles long north to south, and 74 miles wide, east to west. It is so level that the modern towns that are on the lakebed are all within 300 feet of the same elevation. Highway 17 that goes from the north edge of the ancient lakebed to Alamosa is called the Gun Barrel. For more than twenty miles it doesn't have a turn, nor does it have a hill or ravine.

The Rio Grande River heads in the San Juan Mountains and flows into the Valley near the west edge of the old Lake Alamosa to empty out of the Valley at the southeast edge into New Mexico. In the region where the river flows into the valley is a large alluvial plain caused by thousands of years of flooding by the river. On that alluvial plain is the richest soil of the valley. Also, in the western and central region of the valley, water wells are artesian. The Alamosa Formation underlies the surface soil and its bottom layer is clay that formed when the lake held water. A hundred feet of soils have accumulated

The Gun Barrel Highway, Colorado 17. (Photograph from Wikipedia)

above the clay since the lake drained. The clay formed during the lake's existence and acts as a cap on water held beneath it. The drainage from the surrounding mountains goes beneath the clay formation and is under pressure. In some regions of the valley, when wells are drilled into the aqueduct beneath the clay, the water rises to the surface, no pump necessary—an artesian well.

The aqueduct holds a lot of water, so much that the Denver metropolitan area, a perennial growth region that is always looking for water to accommodate growth, wants San Luis Valley water. The most recent plan was to build a pipeline over Poncha Pass to the north and take 30,000 acre-feet of water from the Valley. Locals have been fighting such grandiose plans to transfer their water for Denver's growth for many years. But the adage "money talks" is at play with these relatively poor residents of the Valley.

Flat lake bed land and Mount Blanca in eastern San Luis Valley in the background. (Photograph by Joy Keown)

"If we just had water," was the reaction from those who tried to settle in the eastern portion of the San Luis Valley. I was told by a lady who, with her husband, farms successfully in the Blanca area, "Were it not for our irrigation water, it would take 30 acres to raise a cow." But just after the turn of the 19th century, the San Luis Valley Land Company made plans to put water on the land. The San Luis Valley has been advertised by Chambers of Commerce as the largest alpine valley in the world, and it was seen in the early 1900s by land developers as wide open for new communities, farms, and employment in the towns.

Now, back to the Keown's first acquaintance with San Luis Valley. It was in July of 1908. Their lottery ticket for land where the new town of Blanca was plotted gave them a town lot. The San Luis Land Company guaranteed each ticket holder five acres of land, and a perpetual water right. But in 1908, the irrigation water was not yet there. Two irrigation reservoirs were not near completion.

Granddad's family was not a winner in the land drawing, so with five acres and a lot in the new town they contemplated making a living. There was enthusiasm for the future of the new community as owners waited for the completion of the two reservoirs so water could be put on the land.

The Thomas Keown family were among the most optimistic. Knowing their five acres would not provide a living, they sold a six-room home in Arkansas City. It was their last Kansas property. With the money, they purchased eighty-five more acres from the San Luis Valley Land Company. Stores were built and businesses began. And yet without farm water, at two years of age, the town was at its zenith, with an estimated population of 1,500. Many were still living in tents, including the Keowns. An event soon after landing in Blanca illustrates well what life in the tent and life in the beginning of Blanca might have been like.

One morning a young friend of my dad's—I don't remember ever being told his name—called from outside the tent. He hollered, "Herald, let's go see the atom-biele." It was an automobile on Main Street and for the community that was horse-powered with wagons and carriages, an automobile was a rarity, the new method of transportation. For his friend Herald, in the tent, there were no doors to knock on, just holler.

Main Street in Blanca, 1910, two years after the town was founded. Note, some residents were still living in tents. The population is estimated to be 1500. In 2017 the population was 392. (From photograph donations to the town of Blanca.)

The Keown's plan was to work in the new town until they would be able to establish businesses. After living in the tent for nearly two years they rented a hotel with the intention of renting rooms. But in 1910, Blanca had three hotels. Owners had built them, anticipating growth and a strong economy in the new town on a main highway through the Valley. The time of their renting the hotel was when the town without agriculture water began to fail. Folks were leaving and Keown's first business venture in Blanca didn't make them a living.

We assume the San Luis Valley Land Company needed to know what the population of the new town might be before planning the grades 1-12 school. Below is a picture of remnants of the school and the gymnasium beside it to the right. They were built in 1909.

The Blanca School where Dad attended classes. He played basketball in the gym. The school was razed in 1972 but the remains of the gym still stand. Today the few students of Blanca attend the Sierra Grande School that is halfway between Blanca and Fort Garland. (Photograph from Shannon Hard)

Though the school was razed in 1972, remnants of the gymnasium remained in 2019 when this photograph was taken. Remains of the Blanca School Gym tell us that it was a unique and impressive building when completed in 1909. It had a full-court gymnasium. The walls were framed with vertical steel beams, with adobe sixteen inches thick between the beams. Let us hope it remains as a monument to those who came to Blanca with dreams of building a thriving community. (Photograph by Joy Keown, May, 2019)

According to Dad, in his mother's mind, six years old was too young for children to begin school, so both Dad and Urban began school when they were seven. In 1908, Dad entered the seventh grade in the temporary school that was in a Blanca Main Street building. The new school and a gymnasium were under construction. A new school and the town with 1,500 residents in 1910 must have given the townspeople great hope. But in the spring of 1910, Thomas and Mary Keown and their two young sons were still living in the tent. During that year they moved to a house and Mary began to make the living, such as it was. She baked bread and pies and sold them from the home. That was their living. There was still no irrigation water for their five acres and most of the villagers were aware that with only five acres to farm and the short growing season, farming would not give families independence. But the Keowns, with their additional eighty-five acres, were prepared—only waiting for the water. For others, consolidation of the tracts would be necessary for a viable farm.

The San Luis Land Company had contracted the Trinchera Canal Company to build the two reservoirs on Trinchera Creek: the San Luis Valley Mountain Home and the Smith reservoirs. Blanca was two years old and the Trinchera Canal Company was failing in their contract to build the reservoirs. Trinchera wanted out.

My granddad and eleven other Blanca men, hopeful for a future in farming, formed the Trinchera Irrigation Company and borrowed $500,000 in bonds to finish the reservoirs. They bought out the canal company, along with its water rights and unfinished dams and canals. They hired the contractors Phillips and O'Gara to finish the reservoirs.

With scrapers and wagons to carry the rock and materials, the contractors and their workers finished the reservoirs and by June of 1912 water was running in the ditches. My dad always told us, "When they got the water on the land it wouldn't grow anything." But being late with the water for holders of acreage or the soil being infertile were not the only reasons the eastern Valley failed to bloom. Research says there were multiple reasons. People were poor and not able to put together several tracts of five acre pieces, and there were unpaid taxes. The $500,000 loan to complete the reservoirs had raised the taxes. Even with water, most lost hope and were moving on. The Keowns were on the cusp of the failing community.

After seven years, Thomas Keown, Mary, and their sons left Blanca. It was 1915. Baking and selling homemade bread and pies was a desperation effort. They couldn't see times getting any better. But causes for their leaving the Valley were more complex. Let me reconstruct the times.

Before leaving, my granddad was elected mayor of Blanca. The possibility of the prohibition of the manufacture and sale of alcohol, maybe even drinking it, was in sight and the entire U.S. population was taking sides.

In the 1912 election for mayor, Thomas Keown was the candidate on the dry ticket. As a member of the Blanca town leaders who formed the Trinchera Irrigation Company and finally had the water flowing in the ditches, he was well known. In the election, T.D. Keown, the dry ticket candidate, was elected.

First, more about prohibition. It didn't come on suddenly, but finally in 1920 it was enacted for the entire U.S. with the Volstead Act, more commonly called the Prohibition Act. It banned the manufacture and sale of alcohol.

It was not without precedence. Prohibition had been tried in some states. First was Maine, where they passed a statewide law against selling alcohol in 1851. Other states followed with the "Maine Laws," but they were always appealed after causing riots and opposition. In 1881, Kansas passed a ban on the sale of alcohol, but in that religiously conservative state it failed there, too.

However, many—especially religionist revivalists—continued to cry for a "dry America."

And support continued to grow in Congress. Political support came with the growth of the Women's Christian Temperance Union and the Anti-Saloon League. These organizations were well financed and important, as they pushed the belief that prohibition of alcohol would: "Help cure crime, strengthen families, and improve the national character." Many proponents of prohibition saw alcohol as the national curse.

For a national prohibition, the 18th Amendment was passed in 1920. There would be no more manufacture and sale of alcohol; but the law didn't ban people from drinking the stuff. Immediately, the manufacture and sale went underground. The market remained. For about a decade, enforcement of the "noble experiment," as it came to be called, kept the country dry, or as history shows, tried to keep the country dry. But long before Amendment 18 came, the country was choosing sides. Many communities were split, wet and dry, and Blanca was one of them. And Thomas Keown was its mayor.

At the beginning of the school year in 1910 Dad was fourteen and would be in the eight grade as the school year began. His younger brother, Urban, entered the second grade.

Even before 1910 my dad had caught what my Grandmother Mary may have believed was a fever. It was baseball. It had become the American game, the national pastime. It probably evolved as a hybrid game of town ball and the English game of cricket. Town ball and cricket were played by the elite in the eastern most cities. But baseball, the hybrid, was for the public, men of all occupations: butchers, plumbers, storekeepers, railroaders, and it soon became the entertainment for Sundays for the town of Blanca, too.

Fans are leaving the "Baseball Special" at San Acacio for the game between Alamosa and San Acacio. (Photograph from Fort Garland Museum)

To understand baseball and its hold and effect on American society, there needs to be a special note. In the second half of the nineteenth century, baseball spread. Soldiers in the Civil War played it. Soon every little town in America had baseball fever. Towns unified around the town team. Walt Whitman and Herman Melville, in the last half of the century, wrote poems about America's game. The author, John Thorn, tells about the poets and baseball in his essay, "Whitman, Melville, and Baseball." Whitman followed the evolution of the game throughout his life. But a better description of Whitman's love of the game came in a conversation in 1887 with Horace Traubel, essayist, poet, and magazine publisher. As Traubel reported, Albert Spalding, the pioneer in baseball sports equipment, took a team around the world to introduce America's game. Traubel wrote of the conversation.

Whitman said to Traubel: "Did you see the baseball boys are home from their tour around the world? How I'd like to meet them—talk with them: maybe ask them some questions." Traubel replied, "Baseball is the hurrah game of the republic!" [Whitman] was hilarious: "That's beautiful: the hurrah game! well—it's our game: that's the chief fact in connection with it: America's game: has the snap, go, fling, of the American atmosphere—belongs as much to our institutions, fits into them as significantly as our constitutions, laws: is just as important in the sum total of our historic life." (From *Whitman, Melville, and Baseball* by John Thorn)

Walt Whitman. (Photograph from Library of Congress)

The new town of Blanca and the San Luis Valley had baseball fever. There were no towns excluded. The game was rowdy; trains took teams with fans aboard to opponent towns. And it was played on Sunday afternoons, the Sabbath; the day Mary Keown and most devout Christians believed should be kept holy.

Grandma Keown knew the conflict but did not understand the role of baseball to communities and what it meant to so many, including her sons. American towns, especially those towns developing in the West, it was more than entertainment, it was spirit and identity.

I have never known if Grandma Keown belonged to a particular Christian faith, but without a doubt she was a Christian and tried to live by the religion's principles. That meant for her, and so many others of that time, she had a literal belief in the Bible. At times in her life, through her letters, but especially through her poems and actions, Christianity manifests itself as the guiding light of her life. And she sought it for her family. Here are three verses in her own handwriting of the poem, "My Unworthy Offering," written in Blanca, Colorado on July 16, 1915. Below it, is the typed poem.

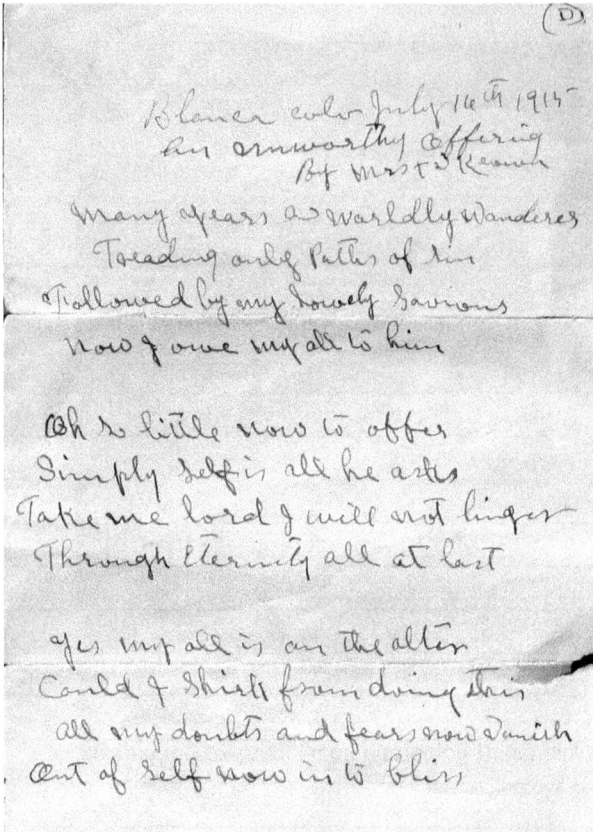

My Unworthy Offering
By Mrs. T D Keown

Many years a Worldly Wanderer
Treading only paths of sin
Followed by my Lovely Saviour
Now I owe my all to him

Oh so little now to offer
Simply self is all he asks
Take me lord I will not linger
Through Eternity all at last

Yes my all is on the altar
Could I Shirk from doing this
All my doubts and fears now vanish
Out of Self now into bliss

Yes mistakes of life so many
Many times by choosing Self
When his promise is so near me
and the path so bright we left

Oh my God accept this offering
Day by day I want to live
Holy Holy yes my Saviour
all to thee I freely give

Shall it be a dying martyr
It would only be like thee
Spare me not this little offer
When at last thy face to see

Oh thy loving face to see

In the summer of 1911, my dad turned fifteen years old and was center fielder for the Blanca town team. He was their youngest player and would enter the ninth grade at the end of summer. He played at the Blanca School, and early on, the town was aware of how well he played the game. He was a modest guy. But as I said previously, throughout his life he would say to me, "I could hit the ball." He was silently so proud, and he deserved to be. But soon after their arrival to Blanca, baseball would be a challenging subject with his mother and dad.

Baseball is a special game. It usually passes from father to son, but to be around it during youth, as my father was, it caught his fascination. He never said his father had interest in the game, but some of the boarders in the Keown's Arkansas City home were players for the Arkansas City semipro team and were his friends.

For Dad's skills and personality, baseball was such a natural. What is it about baseball that it spread from the big cities into rural communities and became America's national game? It has dimensions, special positions for players, and they reside in specific areas. The field is a perfect square, the bases are ninety feet apart and the pitcher stands sixty feet, six inches from home plate. It is a game of complex rules the players must know. Those who play it well, have special talents. Some of the best are fast runners who must run at top speed in seconds to steal a base, or catch a fly ball. They must throw the ball accurately, sometimes 300 feet. And perhaps the most valuable talent to teams is players with the hand-eye coordination it takes to hit the ball. That was Dad's special talent.

In my father's teenage years some major leaguers were known across the country, witness the pitcher Cy Young, basemen Honus Wagner, and the controversial star, Ty Cobb. Dad often spoke of his early baseball heroes.

Even in the small towns of America the talents for baseball are recognized at early ages, and boys are anticipated to be players that will play for the home team and make it better. And the very best may even go on to play baseball at a professional level. Baseball builds fraternity among team members. This must have been the draw and understanding Dad had when he was the center fielder, and the youngest member of the Blanca team.

Many of the players of the San Luis Valley teams drank and smoked and there was betting on the games. To possess a uniform, the invitation to climb on a train and meet another Valley team must have left Dad feeling very special and grownup. But he wasn't grownup, and his mother viewed his sport and its environment as stealing her son's youth. And Sundays were for church and holiness behaviors.

But leaving the conditions of Blanca was still several years away when Dad was fifteen. When back in Blanca School in the ninth grade at fifteen with classmates who were mostly fourteen, he must have been uncomfortable. His Blanca baseball teammates were through with school. Come the next spring when baseball began at the school, he knew he had played baseball at a higher level than any other person in his school. When the town team began to practice for the upcoming Valley games, he was the seasoned center fielder.

In June of 1912, Dad turned sixteen and took the train to play in Alamosa, a town of more than 3,000. He was older and stronger and could hit the home run, which made him an even more important player for the team. In the fall my father went back to Blanca School, but that would be the last year of formal schooling. The family understood. They needed him to work and help keep them afloat. Come summer, on a main canal for the Trinchera Irrigation Company, with a young Hispanic fellow, they became ditch riders. Most ditch riders ride horses, but the two were ditch walkers on the main canal. Their duty was to walk the canal and remove obstructions that impeded the flow, while making sure the flow from the canal headed toward farms were set according to the amount of water the farmer was due. It was a long walk each day and the company had a cabin near the end of the canal where they slept and ate their breakfast before beginning their long daily ditch walk. They returned for dinner in the evening at the cabin. A road came near the cabin and the irrigation company delivered weekly groceries to the men. The "fudge story" about life as a ditch walker needed sixty-two years to conclude.

After the summer of 1975, my dad told the "fudge story" often. When Dad and his partner were ditch walkers, one evening they decided to stir up a pan of fudge. I don't know if they had a recipe, but they put the chocolate mix in a pan and waited for it to become firm. But it didn't harden and remained liquid. For fudge, it was a failure and they placed the pan with the chocolate liquid mix, stirring spoon included, on a shelf in the kitchen area of the one-room cabin. Sixty-some years later Mother and Dad retired (Dad first), and they decided to visit their early homelands. From their home in Cortez, Colorado, they headed east to Kansas and Missouri. Blanca was their first stop, about 250 miles from Cortez. Roads around Blanca are few and Dad found the road that went to the cabin. The small building was still there. They walked over to the cabin that was without a door but still upright and sturdy; they stepped right in. There on that kitchen shelf was the failed fudge pan. My dad took it from the shelf and the spoon was still in it as it had been left more than sixty years before. He always smiled when he said, "The fudge had finally hardened."

The Homestead Act of May 20, 1862 was the first act that enabled land acquisition from the public domain with no cost except filing fees. The concept behind the Homestead Act was to facilitate the growth of an agrarian society by encouraging free farmers, as opposed to slave-based agriculture. With the Civil War won, and the slavery issue removed, the government could pursue such an approach to land acquisition. The act went into effect on January 1, 1863, the same day that President Lincoln signed the Emancipation Proclamation.

The act enabled anyone of at least twenty-one years of age, or the head of a family, including single women and the freed slaves, to acquire up to 160 acres of land from the public domain. An entrant had to file a claim, reside on the land for five years, build a home, make improvements, and farm the land. He or she also had to be a citizen or acquire citizenship prior to satisfying the entry requirements. In return, the entrant would receive a patent transferring the property from the public domain to the private individual.

In 1909 came the Enlarged Homestead Act. It was enacted to facilitate dry-land farming in all western states except California. Lands suitable for settlement under the Act were classified as such by the General Land Office and excluded irrigable lands and land with timber or valuable minerals. Up to 320 acres of land could be acquired under the Enlarged Homestead Act.

By 1915, Dad was nineteen and working in the railroad shop in Alamosa where he would become a close friend of Burt Elam, a fellow about his age. Burt was aware that the area around Dove Creek, Colorado, was open for homesteading with the Enlarged Homesteading Act. My father and Burt Elam were not yet old enough to file for a homestead, but Thomas Keown was. My father took the news to his dad. With Burt, the two went to check out the Dove Creek homesteading. The closest town the Rio Grande Southern Railroad would get them to Dove Creek was Dolores, and there were still thirty-five miles west on a dirt road to reach Dove Creek. Their report to Dad's parents in Blanca must have been optimistic, or at least an alternative to their failed Blanca experience. Soon Thomas Keown filed on a homestead at the Durango General Land Office and the family of four planned their departure from the community of Blanca.

The General Land Office in Durango, Colorado, administered homesteading in the Dove Creek area in 1915. Dove Creek, the unincorporated community, was only four buildings, eighty-two miles west of Durango.

Durango 09611

4—1023.

The United States of America,

To all to whom these presents shall come, Greeting:

WHEREAS, a Certificate of the Register of the Land Office at Durango, Colorado, has been deposited in the General Land Office, whereby it appears that full payment has been made by the claimant Thomas D. Keown according to the provisions of the Act of Congress of April 24, 1820, entitled "An Act making further provision for the sale of the Public Lands," and the acts supplemental thereto, for the southwest quarter of Section one in Township forty-one north of Range nineteen west of the New Mexico Meridian, Colorado, containing one hundred sixty acres,

The upper half of the certificate that granted Thomas D. Keown ownership of his homestead is shown above. With his family they made the required improvements for the transfer of the public land to his possession. The General Land Office in Durango administered the Homestead Act and oversaw the surveying, platting and sale of the public lands in the region.

Again, the Keowns were off for another adventure in a relatively unsettled country where there would be many unknowns. For Granddad Keown it was a late life adventure. He was sixty-four. In 1915 for white males born in 1852, life expectancy in the U.S. was forty-one.

2

THE HOMESTEAD YEARS AT DOVE CREEK

A surveyor from the General Land Office surveyed the homestead plot for Thomas Keown in 1915. It was located about seven dirt-road miles northwest of Dove Creek. Dove Creek at that time had a Post Office in the Parley Butts Mercantile Store.

Parley Butts Mercantile was built in Dove Creek in 1914. In 1915 it also became Dove Creek's first Post Office and in 1946, it was the County Seat of Dolores County. The County Seat was moved from the shrinking mining town of Rico to Dove Creek. (Photograph by Maxine Newell)

As a fifteen-year-old boy in 1877, Parley Butts was in the Hole in the Rock Ward of Mormons who crossed southern Utah canyons to settle in southeastern Utah. President of the LDS Church, Brigham Young, called for settling in the West. John Taylor, Young's successor, called for the southern Utah crossing. The wagon train adventure was to last six weeks, but it took six months. (Photograph from Bluff Fort Visitor Center)

When the Keowns came to Dove Creek country, one of the few structures standing was a small log cabin on the west bank of Dove Creek. It should have been preserved because it would now be a celebrated landmark. It was where Zane Grey lived for a short while as he began his most famous novel, *Riders of the Purple Sage*. It was the only building standing in 1912, where later the town would be.

It was a line camp cabin built by cattlemen. Line camp cabins were built for cattlemen and their herders to shelter while cattle grazed the grass of the plains. There are doubters, but Grey's sidekick and guide in the Dove Creek region was Tom Meyers, step-uncle of my good friend, Glen Baer. Glen was my public school classmate in Rico and Cortez and is an important contributor to this book.

Tom Meyers's stepfather, Billy Meadows, owned and ran trading posts on the Navajo Reservation. Glen's mother, Allie, was born at the Meadow Trading Post south of Shiprock, New Mexico in 1902. Tom Meyers was her stepbrother, who was born to Allie's mother, Anna, in a previous marriage.

Tom lived for a time in McElmo Canyon that borders Ute Mountain, only fifteen miles north of the Four Corners Monument. The mountain is Ute Indian country on the Towaoc Ute Indian Reservation. On to the west of McElmo Canyon is Ismay Trading Post and Hatch Trading Post, both on the north end of the Navajo Reservation.

As a young cowboy, Tom Meyers knew Navajos and Utes. Probably, like his dad, he spoke the Navajo language. Who better would lead Grey through the sage to the Navajo Indian lands that border Dolores County? In 1912 the Great Sage Plain of the western end of the county was cattle country, though grass for cattle grazing is generally sparse and sage dominates. But it was largely untrammeled sage plains. Where better for ideas to bloom for Grey's novel than to headquarter for a time at the Dove Creek cabin? And I might add, *Riders of the Purple Sage*, is a novel about a gunslinger that saves Jane Withersteen, a beautiful ranch woman, from having to marry a Mormon elder against her will. Dove Creek is only ten miles from Utah's most conservative Mormon country. Zane Grey's sage plain guide, Tom Meyers, died young at twenty-one, when he caught the 1918 influenza while serving in World War I.

On their father's new homestead, my dad was nineteen and Urban was thirteen. The rules of claiming a patent deed to the land were to build a home and farm the land, along with other improvements. My sister, Beverly, and I do not know where money for the home came from, except to say that the Keowns were frugal, which is an understatement. A home was of the first order, as they needed a place to live. The home still stands, though it has not been lived in during my memory. When I first saw it, I was eleven years old in 1947, and there it stood, even in 2019, as I remembered it. Wheat crops surround the wooded draw.

The original house still stands. It was built in 1915 on the Thomas Keown homestead. It is only a shell, but much as I remember it when I first saw it in 1947. (Photograph by Joy Keown, July, 2019)

Farming the land was required not only for food to eat but to secure the homestead. Where, on fertile dry land, wheat and pinto bean crops are today, in 1915 it was sagebrush. Sagebrush is a woody species of the genus Artemisia and well rooted. It is the dominant plant species from the LaPlata Mountains west of Durango, Colorado to Monticello, Utah. Topographers call those rolling plains, the Great Sage Plains. The Sage Plain was a more applicable and realized name before farmers and ranchers cleared the sage from the land for farms and ranches.

Before the Keowns were to claim a homestead, plow and farm, the sagebrush had to be removed. The family all joined the clearing for planting field corn. They were not tractor farmers. Today, caterpillar tractors would make short work of the sage, but for them it was hard handwork and long days with grubbing hoes.

The land planned for farming was mostly covered with sagebrush that was removed by hand with a grubbing hoe, as shown below. (Photograph by Joy Keown)

A five-pound grubbing hoe. (Wikipedia free photos)

When I was a junior high school principal in Blanding, Utah to the southwest of Dove Creek, my parents came to see us. I showed Dad the native plants I had transplanted on the school campus. I wanted the students to know their native plants. I'm a biologist and my field is ecology, though for a few years I was the school principal. Dad asked me why I planted sagebrush. He said he was paid a dollar a day by homesteader neighbors to grub it out.

Field corn on the homesteads wasn't an experiment, but to raise it on the dry lands depended on rains. The Anasazi culture, nearly two thousand years before the homesteaders, raised corn on the same sage lands. But for homesteaders, the crop was for more than to eat. It was to sell, for a living.

At Hovenweep National Monument, the Anasazi raised corn. The Keown homestead was twenty-five miles to the north. The Dakota Sandstone outcrops here at the monument. (Hovenweep National Monument Photography Gallery)

Varieties of Anasazi corn are raised today. However, the ears today are much larger than the Anasazi corn ears we find in their ruins, even accounting for more than fifteen hundred years or more of shriveling. (Photograph from Lupine Knoll Farm)

The towns and farms from the La Plata Mountains east of Cortez, Colorado, one hundred miles west to Monticello, Utah, nearly eighty miles, lie atop the Dakota Sandstone Formation originating about 70 million years ago. The best soils of the region are red-brown loess soils. They are aeolian sediment formed by the accumulation of wind-blown silt.

The Monument Valley region to the south is their source. They are at the surface in large regions where the southwest winds have been depositing the weathered sandstone for millions of years. Dakota Sandstone is the bedrock. The fertile red–brown soils were the soils of most of the Dove Creek homesteads. But the Dove Creek region farms that stretched to twelve miles west from Cortez were without water, except for rains.

Today, the large Dolores River Project provides irrigation water west to the town of Cahone, nine miles east of Dove Creek. The homesteaders, like the Anasazi, depended upon rains. Cortez and farmers in Montezuma Valley have had an irrigation system from the Dolores River, built about 1900. But their soils were not red-brown. Homesteaders got the name, "dry landers."

Raising corn as a money crop, and farming with a team of horses on the arable soil, was always a gamble; even more unreliable than is most farming.

My dad couldn't speak of raising dry land corn on the homestead without talking about the "rabbit problem"—Jackrabbits, (Black Tailed Jackrabbits, *Lepus californicus*). A new crop of corn pushing through the ground drew jackrabbits. In fact, Dad said in the spring when the crop was young, it was possible to walk the perimeter of the crop in the morning and see the swath the rabbits had eaten in the night. Those first years, before Dad, and much later his brother Urban, began going to the San Juan Mountains mines and mills to work and support the farm, the corn was their life. Rabbits were truly a plague. To shoot them was Dad's and Urban's protection for the corn. They used 22-caliber rifles and 22 long rifle bullets and a flashlight. He said he would sometimes walk most of the night and kill a dozen or more rabbits.

The homestead story of shooting rabbits cannot be told without including the family dog, Shep, or "One-Shot Shep," as Dad often called him. Shep was a partner in shooting rabbits. He would be at Dad's heel as they circled the field and wouldn't leave his place beside Dad, even when the rabbit was spotted and Dad had it in his rifle sight. But with the first shot, off went Shep. It was Shep's turn for the rabbit. Dad said of Shep's partnership in rabbit hunting, "You always had to get the rabbit on the first shot."

Our dad always told us that protecting the corn was why he was such a good shot. I'm sure shooting rabbits was his practice, but later in the Army I learned that the reason he could shoot so well was the same reason he could "hit the baseball." It was his hand-eye coordination.

On Sundays when I was a kid, we often went to my Granddad Gage's farm, five miles west of Dove Creek. If relatives were not there, Dad and I would hunt rabbits. We often ate the cottontails or if we shot a jack rabbit, the dog(s) got it. Though I shot "expert" in the Army, I could never shoot with Dad, even when he became old. When relatives were there at the farm, often we placed cans out away from the front yard, about forty yards. It was a friendly contest for the males. I've heard Uncle Fay say jokingly, "I'm not shooting if Herald is shooting."

Farming corn did not pay a living for the Keown family of four and they soon changed the crop to wheat. The Keowns planted with horses. Horses were what Thomas Keown knew. He loved them but his sons were not experienced wheat farmers, as was their Dad, who had been a Kansas wheat farmer. The rabbits were not the noticeable problem as they were with corn, though I'm certain they continued to take their toll. The corn was harvested by hand but harvesting a wheat crop, even a small one, brought in a crew with a threshing machine. Pictured below are all of the elements of raising the wheat at the homestead: horses for plowing and planting, and the threshing crew that made the rounds to the wheat farms.

The wheat threshing crew on the Keown homestead. Notice the large water tank. The engine ran with a steam engine. When the job was done, Dad hired on with the crew and helped thresh wheat in the area, and even into the Montezuma Valley to the east. (Photograph from the trunk)

Before the story of Cowling's well, it is time to paint a picture of the community of Dove Creek homesteaders. Most landed at their homesteads in similar circumstances: poor, unacquainted with neighbors to be.

In front of the Brown's tarpaper covered cabin are the Browns and the Keowns, minus my uncle Urban. From left is Dad, Grandma Keown, Mrs. Brown, Granddad Keown, and General Brown. (Photograph is from the trunk)

General Brown wasn't named General because he was a "take charge" guy. Dad and his family were often helping the Browns to make a go of it. Browns raised pigs in a pen that was made of pinion and juniper trees laid horizontal and it was so large that the pigs were wild beyond the behavior of most domestic swine. So, come time to kill and butcher a porker, General Brown called on Dad. Knowing Dad's reputation for marksmanship, Mr. Brown asked if Dad would shoot one of the pigs. Dad said the hogs were so wild he had a hard time getting within twenty yards, but he killed the pig with one shot from his 22-caliber rifle. The shot was just above the eyes and the pig went right down. General Brown told Dad, "The shot should have been right between the eyes." General Brown's knowledge of shooting and guns was nil. He didn't know the business end of a rifle. With the help of neighbors, the pig was butchered.

Thirty years later when our family lived in Cortez, the Browns had moved to a small home in south Cortez. They continued to call on Dad for help with chores that most town residents would have been able to accomplish. Dad was his kind and helpful self and always gave the Browns the help they needed.

Of course, the homesteaders needed domestic water, be it carried from a well near the home or hauled from a friendly neighbor's well. The Cowlings were a homesteading family that probably were better heeled than most Dove Creekers. They first landed in southwestern Colorado at Cortez. The missus was an optometrist and they set up her shop in Cortez. Perhaps they only wanted the homestead experience when they left Cortez for a dry-land farm. Their homestead was near the Keowns.

The Cowlings needed a well, and with most homesteaders it didn't call for bringing in a drilling rig. Most homestead wells of the area were hand dug wells in draws near the home. Hand dug wells are large relatively shallow holes made to reach the ground water. The Cowlings first called in a driller with a hammer drill and he struck ground water, but he kept on drilling to reach more water in deeper strata below the Dakota Sandstone. But then a problem occurred. The bit was stuck down deep and for three days it couldn't be retrieved. Of course, because of this a pipe to the water and a hand pump could not be installed.

The Cowlings then decided to settle for a hand well, so they brought in a fellow who knew the process and digging a hand well commenced. The primary tools for digging a hand well are a shovel and a pick. Of course, there was no guarantee there would be water. Even today, whether the hole is dug with a shovel or a modern rotary drilling rig, there's no guarantee.

Dad told the story of when he helped to dig the Cowling's hand well at the Cortez Library when he was eight-six years old, just a year before he died. He was asked to tell of pioneering in Dolores County by Tom Johnson, a local newspaper reporter who knew of Dad's history and memory. From the tape of his library stories, I have considerable detail about the Cowling well digging experience.

Mrs. Cowling hired Dad to help the fellow in charge of digging the hand well. He was paid two dollars a day, not good but not bad for the time. The well site was chosen in a draw near the Cowling's home. Digging the well required a couple of sturdy poles secure in the ground on the sides of the hole, a crossbar, a pulley for the crossbar, a large bucket and a strong rope, like the setup shown in the two photos below. In Dad's day, if the well hole was deep a horse or mule pulled up the bucket full of dirt and rock. A hand dug well in the beginning is shown below. Upon completion, a hand dug well may look like the one in the next photograph.

The digging of a hand dug well begins. (Google, free images, hand dug wells)

A hand dug well completed. (Google, free images, hand dug wells)

The bucket for dirt and rock raised from the Cowling well hole was made from the bottom half of a fifty-five gallon barrel. A bail was installed on the barrel half and a large rope was tied to the bail. It was threaded through the pulley on the crossbar. The rope went out to the harness on a horse that pulled up the large improvised bucket.

The fellow in charge of construction of the well was digging in the hole with Dad and they would fill the bucket, holler to Mrs. Cowling, who would get the horse to pull up the bucket. Then they would climb the ladder, swing the full bucket to the side, empty it and climb back down the ladder to continue filling the empty bucket. Mrs. Cowling's role was to back the horse up to lower the bucket and ready the horse to pull up another full bucket. The well digging was going as planned until Mrs. Cowling was lowering the bucket back into the hole and backed the horse too far. The horse went into the hole. Dad said the guy in charge saw the horse coming and he went up the ladder like "a squirrel goes up a tree."

Dad said with the horse upright in the hole there was just room for himself, the ladder and the horse. He managed to get on the ladder, climb out and the helpless horse was left upright but standing on its rear hooves in the hole. It appeared the horse was unharmed, though horses do not normally stand for long on their rear hooves. Neighbors were needed, all who they could quickly summon. A tarp was used as a sling. Hank Snyder was a neighbor with a team of mules. Down the ladder went the guy with the sling, ropes tied to the corners. Soon the sling was under the belly and the Snyder mules were lifting the horse, using the pulley, to where its front hooves had traction on the ground at the edge of the hole. It walked off "with only a few scratches," Dad said. That was all the well drilling for the day and Dad said he told Mrs. Cowling he was through with the project. But this is not the end of the story.

Dad said he really needed the two dollars a day and after a couple of days he went back to work for Mrs. Cowling. Interestingly, he never spoke about Mr. Cowling's role in the well story.

The shovel digging only went a few feet deeper before they hit bedrock. Whether the hole had become too deep to use the ladder and the ladder remained in the hole I don't know, but Dad and the guy in charge were riding out of the hole in the horse-drawn bucket. Bedrock called for dynamite, fuses, caps and holes being drilled by hand with a hammer and rock chisel into the sandstone for loading the powder.

Dad never talked about where he learned how to use explosives, and this was before his mining days. The two well diggers dug holes in the bedrock, loaded the holes with dynamite containing the fuse, and gently tamped dirt into the loaded holes to contain the blast. The fellow in charge of the well was out of the hole and handling the horse. Dad lit the fuses, climbed into the bucket and hollered, "Fire in the hole!"

The bucket didn't move. "The fuses were spitting," Dad said. But the horse wouldn't pull the rope. Dad was ready for the alternative way out of the hole, which might have been climbing the rope, when his partner hit the horse in the butt with a stick. He took off with a leap and ran. Dad came up the hole in the bucket, "Just like I was riding a rocket," he said. The bail on the bucket hit the pulley as Dad leaped for the edge of the hole. He walked away from the hole from where the blast would soon happen. Then he walked up to the Cowling's house and told Mrs. Cowling for the second and final time, "No more well digging for me."

World War I began in Europe on July 28, 1914. The United States joined its allies, Britain, France and Russia, in the war on April 6, 1917. The war ended November 11, 1918. The Keowns prided themselves on their good citizenship and patriotism. At the end of farming season in 1917 Dad joined the Navy. His service was a year and a month. As the old song told the story for so many young men from the farms, "You're in the Army (Navy for Dad) now, you aren't behind the plow..."

Herald Keown at age twenty-one in the Navy during World War I. (Photograph is from the trunk)

Herald Garrison Keown was immediately assigned to the U.S.S. Supply ship. It was old when the U.S. joined the First World War. Built in 1873, the vessel had been decommissioned first at the U.S. Navy Yard in New York in April of 1889. But with the Spanish American War it was refurbished and commissioned again and sailed near Cuba. But that war was the United States' shortest war, April 21, 1898–August 1898.

Having been refurbished, the ship's service to the Navy continued. With the Spanish American War, the U.S. acquired possessions in the Philippines and Spanish America and the U.S.S. Supply served the nation in both areas. In particular, the Panama Canal was very important in both World Wars. It was the site of the major portion of Dad's naval time. Below is the picture of the U.S.S. Supply that he brought home from the war, and below it is the crew he served with on that ship.

The U.S.S. Supply that served the Navy in two wars. It was built in 1873 and the Navy purchased it used, twenty-six years old. They refurbished it twice. Its second and final decommissioning was September 15, 1919. (Photograph from the author's wall)

Herald Keown is the large sailor in the middle of the second row and adjoining the small sailor in the second row to his left. The picture was taken at the bow of the U.S.S. Supply. (Photograph from the author's wall)

On June 13th, before joining the Navy, Dad turned twenty-one, and that was old enough to file for a homestead. So, in Durango he filed the application for 160 acres adjoining his dad's homestead. While in the Navy, he was exempt by the General Land Office from making the improvements required of homesteaders.

The year plus a month in the Navy was very impressionable, even life-changing for Dad. He was robust and strong, six feet and he weighed 190 pounds. The average weight of a World War I U.S. sailor was only 112 pounds and only five feet five inches tall. The hard physical work Dad had known showed with his physique. While in the Navy he boxed heavyweight. It was a natural sport for a man of his reach and reactions. An incident he told me about says so much about his character, his perception of himself, and his acknowledgment of his physical superiority.

Sailors slept in hammocks on the ship. Once he was sleeping while other sailors in the area were awake. A smaller sailor lacking good judgment, and probably wanting to impress others with his bravery, cut the single rope at the foot of Dad's hammock. Dad slid to the deck starting with his feet. Sailors in the area didn't get the reaction expected from their mate. They said, "Take him Herald." As Dad got up, he eyed the prankster who was probably expecting a fight. Dad said to the smaller guy, "You made a mistake and you know it." That was it.

The reaction of my father was as I would expect. It left his audience disappointed but admiring his composure and maturity. The offense was infantile and gained the offender no esteem. Dad was already a man, caring for aging parents and a younger brother. He had adult responsibilities since he was sixteen and he would be returning to his homestead responsibilities. In so many ways he was older than his sailor mates. As a kid growing up I watched how he was accepted and stood out in a group. His presence was naturally acknowledged.

At our home in Cortez our dad could touch the eight-foot ceiling with all five fingers. I'm six foot-one and I could barely touch the ceiling. And for leg length, his legs were proportional to his arms. When walking, he could leave us all behind. One time at Grandpa Gage's, a good gesture by Grandpa was to give us gasoline for our car, gasoline that grandpa purchased at the farmer's discount. Farmers didn't pay the tax. It was stored in a barrel and using a hand pump, Grandpa pumped the gas from the barrel to our car. But the gas had water in it. The car wouldn't start. With a gas can, Dad and I began the five-mile walk to Dove Creek. I was about eleven or twelve years old and skipping to keep up. Before we reached the mailbox, about a quarter of a mile, I turned back, so I wouldn't slow him down.

But back to the Navy. He talked about the Panama Canal which for the time, and still is, an astonishing feat of physics, engineering and construction. Like so many men of his time, the armed services were the only time they would ever leave the states. To Panama with the Navy was the only time Dad ever left the U.S. and those events stayed with him. It was good for him that there were no battle events. But he told of several experiences that stayed with him. One was about the young men of Panama who would dive for coins from the dock where the U.S.S. Supply was anchored. I don't know how deep the water was in the bay where the ship was docked, though I have been there. Panama boys would dive for coins that sailors would throw from the ship and retrieve them from the bottom of the bay. It was to my father (and it seems to me), to be an extraordinary swimming accomplishment. The dive must have been at least twenty or thirty feet. What a feat to dive to the depth of the coin, find it, and get back to the surface. The ship was more than three hundred feet long. How deep was the water to keep the ship off of the bottom? What was the Panamanian economy and employment that the boys would make the dive for a nickel, dime, or a quarter?

Dad got the mumps just before the U.S.S. Supply was to sail to the Pacific. The disease is very contagious, and he had to go ashore for his own health and to protect the crew aboard. On another ship he came back to the states and landed in New York.

It was announced on ship that all sailors could pick up a free pass and attend a New York Yankees game. The great attraction for everyone was Babe Ruth. To make the game even more memorable for the sailors and fans, Babe Ruth hit a homerun.

The Great Bambino was beginning a career that would eclipse many records of the time. Some still hold today. Hitting more than forty home runs in eleven seasons hasn't been equaled. Before Ruth, hitting thirty home runs in one season was the record. Ruth hit sixty and the record stood for many years.

Dad lived for baseball, even though during the first years at Dove Creek he had to let it go. There weren't enough players in the region to form a team, but that situation wouldn't last long.

And those World War I songs stuck with Dad. He liked to sing and could carry a tune. It was always around breakfast time that he broke into song. I remember the words he sang to "Someday I'm Going to Murder the Bugler."

> I met a soldier friend of mine in town
> the other day
> I asked him how he liked the life
> and this is what he said
> Someday I'm going to murder the bugler,
> someday they're going to find him dead
> And then I'll get that other pup, the one that
> wakes the bugler up
> And spend the rest of my life in bed.

Then there was the song that went with the war that most folks were humming, "Over There." It was that middle verse that was so popular that Dad often sang.

> Over there, over there
> Send the word, send the word over there
> That the Yanks are coming
> The Yanks are coming
> The drums rum-tumming
> everywhere

So prepare, say a prayer
Send the word, send the word to beware
We'll be over, we're coming over
And we won't come back till it's over
over there.

3

SAVED BY THE COLORADO MINES

When Dad returned from the War his folks on the homestead seemed much older, though it was just over a year he'd been gone. Maybe it was because of his company with the youthful companions in the service. His brother, Urban, was sixteen and had finished his schooling. Dove Creek didn't have a high school. It was plain to see that farming the homesteads would not support the family of four. There was work in the San Juan Mountain's mines and mills or on the railroad that linked the mines and the towns together. The San Juan Mountains were where many able homesteaders went to supplement, or continue, dry land farming.

Dad's first mine work out of the Navy was at La Plata City, Colorado, where he drove an ore haul truck. The heyday for La Plata City and nearby Parrott City along the La Plata River was in the late nineteenth century. Until 1885, when the county seat was moved to Durango, Parrott City was the county seat of La Plata County. By the 1920s mining along the La Plata was waning.

Dad never told me where he learned to drive but it was a time for men (women drivers came later, including Grandma Keown) to transition from horses to autos and trucks. At La Plata City he lived in a bunkhouse. La Plata City was—it is a ghost town now—near the headwater of the La Plata River, about twelve miles north of the small community of Hesperus. Dad's truck-driving job was to haul ore from a mine to dump the load at Hesperus into a train car waiting on the Rio Grande Southern Railroad (RGSR) tracks. The employment with the mills, mines, and the railroad was during fall and wintertime. He remained a farmer in the late spring and summers during the early 1920s.

Dad was returning with an empty dump truck to a La Plata City mine following a snowstorm and the dirt road was slick with packed snow. The stretch before the mine was steep with a very long drop off into the La Plata River Canyon on his right side. The truck began to spin out and then was sliding backward. For Dad, it was an immediate decision to prevent the truck from gaining backward speed, his losing control and perhaps going into the canyon. The brakes were useless. He turned the truck into the dirt bank on the inward side of the road. It went up the steep bank and remained vertical and upright, but not for long. It fell onto its cab, onto the road. Dad was on his head in the cab, but able to get out. Like so many of his stories, I don't remember that he ever finished his recollection of the experience: how the truck was up righted; if he continued as a truck driver with another truck; what his next job was, or whether it was at La Plata City.

I think he liked working on the railroad. Often the railroad work was maintaining or building trestles that were numerous along the mountainous Rio Grande tracks. He was often overnight in Ridgway, Telluride, Rico, Dolores, Silverton or Durango. The crew spent nights in railroad coaches near depots along the route. It was always physical work, from which he never shied away.

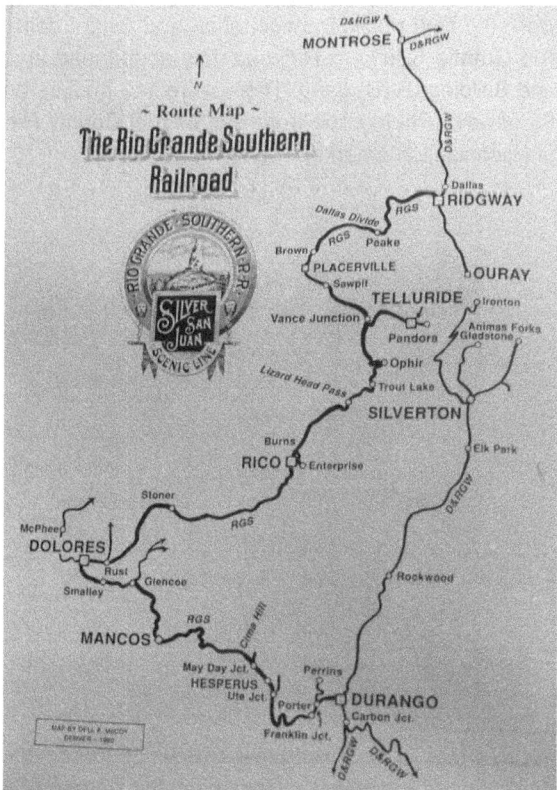

The route of the Rio Grande Southern railroad tied southwestern Colorado mining towns together. Note that rails never connected Silverton and Ouray. If one travels Highway 40 between the two towns, the lack of a rail connection is obvious. That section of Highway 40 is the Million Dollar Highway. The mountains are so rugged a railroad would have been cost prohibitive. (Map is from *The Rio Grande Southern Story*, Volume 5)

This is a Galloping Goose as it crossed the Trout Lake Trestle (#51A) between Rico and Telluride. Several of the Galloping Gooses (converted trucks with a bus and trailer) were the final public transportation and freight delivery vehicles on the railroad. The Rio Grande Southern Railroad was abandoned in 1952. Dad worked on the Bridge and Building (B&B) gang. There were 140 bridges and trestles between Durango and Ridgeway. (Photograph from San Miguel County Historical Register and Designation of Historical Landmarks)

Today's relic of the Trout Lake Trestle. Of the dozens that existed between Durango, Telluride and Ridgeway, excepting on the Durango-Silverton Spur, it is the only one left and has been designated a Colorado Historic site. The other trestles were salvaged for the timbers. (Photograph by Joy Keown, July 2019)

I recall after his and Mom's retirement they rode the now famous Narrow Gauge passenger train from Durango to Silverton. It was a spur of the RGSR. That stretch was preserved and has become the main tourist event for Durango. Side canyon after side canyon and draw after draw, it crosses trestles. Some are very high and excite the passengers. Storyteller that he was, as their passenger car passed over one of the high trestles he said to the stranger riding in the seat next to him, "I remember working on that trestle when I was a young man." It didn't impress the passenger but only triggered the fellow to begin a narrative that to Dad and Mom seemed unending about travels and the many trains he had ridden. Dad discovered the fellow did not want a conversation about the Narrow Gauge train they were on, highlights of its history or his own history with the trestles on the RGSR. He was only interested in glorifying his travels. Dad said, "Did you ever ride the Bridal Veil Tram?"

"What's that?" the windy stranger said.

"It was a ride that took miners and mill workers in ore buckets from the Pandora Mill near Telluride to the electric power plant and mine trails where they were let off to begin a day's work. It is a mile long and it rises two thousand feet in elevation, near the headwaters of the San Miguel River. That was another job I had in these mountains in the 1920s," he told the outsider.

Did it interrupt the stranger's continuous narration of his travel? I don't know. But the Bridal Veil Tram ride to work always had my attention. He later rode the tram with his brother, Urban. It was two men per ore bucket. I remember Urban recalling that when the wind was blowing it caused workers to crouch down in the bucket, as it would swing from side to side, at places two or three hundred feet above the headwaters of the San Miguel River.

The Bridal Veil Tram took ore and men in tram buckets from the Pandora Mill near the large rock in the right hand bottom corner of the photograph to the Smuggler-Union Hydroelectric Plant and to mine trail heads. From the Pandora Mill to the power plant is a mile. The power plant is the building at the left side of the saddle of the mountains. Miners and plant workers would ride on the tram to the Smuggler Power Plant and trailheads that led to the mines beyond. (Photograph by Joy Keown)

Miners are loading the tram bucket for the ride to the Smuggler Mines operations. The tram took miners to the mines and plant workers to the Smuggler-Union Hydroelectric Plant. (Photograph from Telluride Historical Museum)

The power plant and destination of the Bridal Veil Tram. Behind it is Blue Lake that stores water that falls through the turbines in the power plant. The power plant is perched on the rock ledge above Bridal Veil Falls. The Smuggler-Union Hydroelectric Plant was built in 1907 to power the Smuggler-Union Mining Company's mines and mill. (Photograph by Diane Greer, http://www.hikingwalking.com)

Once on a job in the winter at the Smuggler-Union Hydroelectric Plant, Dad was on a walkway behind the power plant over Blue Lake. The lake was the storage water to fall through the generators in the plant. The activity of the plant kept the lake water from freezing near the plant and beneath the walkway. Dad said he was about to slip from the walkway, and he grabbed for any object to keep from falling into the lake. It wasn't just any object. It was a high voltage wire. I don't know if it was the charge of the wire or him jumping away because of the shock, but he fell backward into the lake. He always said those in charge at the plant who helped pull him out of the lake said he was "lucky to be alive." Like so many of his stories, this one comes with the highlight and without much detail, or maybe it is that I don't recall details. It was warm in the power plant where he went following the fall. There was a resident who lived at the plant full time. Was there a change of clothes? Did he go back to work that day?

In 1920, at the time of this photograph, mining in Telluride was beginning to decline. In 1900 mining had been in full swing. (Photograph from *Colorado History*)

In the early years, Telluride was full of working men, mostly single, and there were many bunkhouses where they ate and slept. The first bunkhouse Dad stayed at began with what I guess was a reasonable question by the lady proprietor. Dad asked what the cost would be. "I always wait to see how much you eat," she said. The price must have been agreeable as he stayed there many times when he worked at Telluride in the fall and winter months. He said there was "always a job in Telluride." It took many men (Not many women were in Telluride in those days) to support the mines and mills and the ore going out on the Rio Grande Southern.

Speaking of the shortage of women in Telluride in early mining days, there was not a railroad into the town until 1891. Much of the traffic to the isolated town went over the one lane wagon road over Ophir Pass. It is just east of Ophir, the very small mining town ten miles south of Telluride. It was an Otto Mears toll road. We went over the pass one summer with our four-wheel drive vehicle. At the summit, the original—or maybe it was a duplicate – toll fee sign was posted for tourists to recapture the time and Mears' toll charges. It read: Horses and mules 25 cents, cows fifteen cents, goats ten cents, and women free. In 1881 there were 894 people in Rico and only fifty-four were women.

A worry for Dad and his brother, Urban, was to leave their folks in Dove Creek on the homestead as they worked the mills and mines of the San Juans. The parents were aging. Grandpa Keown was past seventy.

In 1926, Dad bought his folks a car so they would not rely on neighbors for needs, especially should they need medical help. It was a 1924 Chevrolet touring car. I don't know the cost of purchase but the tax receipt I have for county and state tax for the license in 1926 was seventeen dollars. The valuation for the car on the receipt was four hundred fifty dollars. Grandma learned to drive it.

It was a cold winter night while working in Rico. Dad was staying at the Rico Hotel. There wasn't a central heating system in the hotel. Each room had a small stove and a chimney. And with each stove was a bucket of water. Dad stoked the stove with coal for the night and went to bed.

In the night a fire in his room woke him. The fire was where the chimney exited the ceiling of his room. The chimney was red hot. He grabbed the bucket of water and with one heave he threw the entire bucket at the fire and hot chimney. It only took the one bucket and the fire was out. Again, end of story. I guess I should have asked him... Did he build another fire? What was the proprietor's reaction and the reaction of other tenants? Was Dad the only one who woke?

In the twenties, farming was not yet sustainable in the Dove Creek country, as it would become beginning just prior to World War II. My father began to spend less time at farming and more time with employment in the San Juans, especially Rico. Rico had a baseball team, and a good one. Of course, that attracted Dad to Rico for the summers.

He came to know the towns of Rico and Telluride, especially Rico. He knew of their origins and understood what sustained them. He knew of the booms and the busts. The hills were full of the relics and reminders of the town's pasts: old mine dumps at the sides and tops of mountains, some reaching to the streams and the river below, remnants of ore processing mills in the valleys, etc. He told me that the graveyards of the towns were testimony to the short lives mining caused, in particular the early mining days.

Groups of industrialists, men of wealth, speculative rich folks, and many in Europe, funded such structures as the Bridal Veil Tram and the Smuggler-Union Hydro Electric Plant. Many financiers had never seen the towns or structures built where they speculated on rich ore finds with their excesses of money.

The speculation was throughout the Rockies, but especially in Colorado. Even at the turn of the 19th century these structures costs millions, not the kind of money miners could accumulate. Only those with wealth could build a Pandora Mill. But to build and operate such structures required labor, and lots of it. Though my father was at these places in the twenties, it was men like him who earlier built such edifices for the extraction of minerals. I heard him say that the word in Telluride was that when the southern European immigrants left the ships in New York harbor they were illiterate, at least in English, and knew few words of the new language. When asked where they were going, their answer was, "The Smuggler." That may have been the word around early Telluride while the town was booming, but it was not that much of an exaggeration. The Smuggler operations for employment or its contribution to Colorado's economy was enormous. These immigrant men had the message that the Smuggler was paying three dollars a day for labor. And for some miners, payment was for how much ore they would dig from the mountain and load into mine track cars.

The buying power of a 1900 dollar would be nearly thirty dollars in 2020. In the 1900s the wage would equal ninety dollars per day. It would probably have been a great inducement to head west for Telluride. But the money was only part of the story. The "rest of the story," as Paul Harvey used to say, was mostly untold to the immigrants.

Miners had short lives if they mined very long in the silicon rock mines of Telluride and Rico. Death was from silicosis, commonly called "miner's con." Minute particles of silicon rock dust stick in the alveoli of the lungs, disabling each of the thousands of minute oxygen-absorbing structures. Finally, there is not enough lung surface to provide life-giving oxygen. The exact cause was not known in 1900, only the result. It was an acknowledged disease and the health cost that went with getting the gold, silver and other minerals to the mills. And mills were clouded with dust, too.

There are three types of silicosis: chronic, accelerated, and acute. Chronic form emerges ten years after the onset of exposure. The accelerated form develops within a shorter period (four–ten years) after a more intense exposure. Telluride had all three forms and the Telluride graveyard is testimony to hundreds of deaths caused by miner's con.

I was in Telluride in 1971 driving a fifty-five-passenger school bus with thirty-four high school junior and senior students aboard. We were going to walk through the Telluride graveyard to carry out a study. It was an activity in the curriculum of a federal grant program to study natural science phenomena of the Four Corners Country that included human history and cultures of the area.

It was in July and I was a high school sciences teacher at the Monticello High School in Monticello, Utah. If you know the Four Corners Country you might say, as my dad did many times, "The whole area should have been the world's largest national park. It exposes every natural phenomenon known to man." It had been Dad's suggestion that with our students we walk through the Telluride graveyard to see the ages of men who died in the early mining days of that famous mining town. Earlier at Monticello High I took my Human Physiology class to the local graveyard of that town to discover the age at death of those who died before 1920 and those who died after 1950. At Telluride we would find the age at death of men who died before 1920.

Gravestones did not give causes of death, but our results were shocking. I wish I had kept the results. We found few males that ever reached the age of sixty and most were middle aged men, even young men, testimony to the ravages of dry rock mining in silicon rock mines.

This gravestone in the Telluride Cemetery reads: Sven J. Serigstad, 1881–1911, REST IN PEACE. He was thirty years old. (Photograph by Joy Keown, July, 2019)

At the turn of the nineteenth century a forty hour-work week was several decades away and there were no eight-hour days, only the hours the mine owners expected.

But there was more adversity that went with the mining. As the song goes, "It's dark as a dungeon way down in the mine." The light for miners was attached to a hat and fueled by carbide. Battery powered lights are used today.

Miners with carbide lamps of the type used in the hey-day of mining in Rico and Telluride. Carbide lamps are powered by the reaction of calcium carbide with water. This reaction produces acetylene gas which burns a white flame that is reflected on a saucer-like shiny metal disk. (Photograph from the National Museum of American History)

I will end this chapter with an appropriate poem by Robert Service. Service is best known for his poems of the frozen northwest. But with "Song of the Wage-slave," we appreciate the lives of early Rico and Telluride workers. In verse, we hear of the lives of men who carried out the labor for wealthy mine owners who were on another plane.

The Song of the Wage-slave
By Robert W. Service

When the long, long day is over, and the Big Boss gives me my pay,
I hope that it won't be hell-fire, as some of the parsons say.
And I hope that it won't be heaven, with some of the parsons I've met—
All I want is just quiet, just to rest and forget.
Look at my face, toil-furrowed; look at my calloused hands;
Master, I've done Thy bidding, wrought in Thy many lands—
Wrought for the little masters, big-bellied they be, and rich;
I've done their desire for a daily hire, and I die like a dog in a ditch.
I have used the strength Thou hast given, Thou knowest I did not shirk;
Threescore years of labor—Thine be the long day's work.
And now, Big Master, I'm broken and bent and twisted and scarred,
But I've held my job, and Thou knowest, and Thou wilt not judge me hard.
Thou knowest my sins are many, and often I've played the fool—
Whiskey and cards and women, they made me the devil's tool.
I was just like a child with money; I flung it away with a curse,

Feasting a fawning parasite, or glutting a harlot's purse;
Then back to the woods repentant, back to the mill or the mine,
I, the worker of workers, everything in my line.
Everything hard but headwork (I'd no more brains than a kid),
A brute with brute strength to labor, doing as I was bid;
Living in camps with men-folk, a lonely and loveless life;
Never knew kiss of sweetheart, never caress of wife.
A brute with brute strength to labor, and they were so far above—
Yet I'd gladly have gone to the gallows for one little look of Love.
I, with the strength of two men, savage and shy and wild—
Yet how I'd ha' treasured a woman, and the sweet, warm kiss of a child!
Well, 'tis Thy world, and Thou knowest. I blaspheme and my ways be rude;
But I've lived my life as I found it, and I've done my best to be good;
I, the primitive toiler, half naked and grimed to the eyes,
Sweating it deep in their ditches, swining it stark in their styes;
Hurling down forests before me, spanning tumultuous streams;
Down in the ditch building o'er me palaces fairer than dreams;
Boring the rock to the ore-bed, driving the road through the fen,
Resolute, dumb, uncomplaining, a man in a world of men.
Master, I've filled my contract, wrought in Thy many lands;
Not by my sins wilt Thou judge me, but by the work of my hands.
Master, I've done Thy bidding, and the light is low in the west,
And the long, long shift is over ... Master, I've earned it— Rest.

4

BECOMING THE COUNTY TREASURER—BASEBALL'S ROLE

When it was time to farm, come spring in the homestead years, it was back from the San Juan Mountains to the homesteads for the Keown sons. Urban and Dad had missed baseball through those early homestead years, so with other Dove Creekers of baseball yearnings in the early twenties, a team was formed. They were all newcomers to Dove Creek and many homesteaders knew well the entertainment and pleasures of playing the sport. Below is a Dove Creek team of the twenties, uniforms and all. But it wasn't their first Dove Creek team. Urban pitched on the first team.

By 1928 Dove Creek was playing the nearest team of Cahone, Colorado, only nine miles east, and other teams of the Montezuma Valley. Cortez was the largest community in the region. Urban is farthest to the left and Dad is second standing on the left. At least one team member is missing. (Photograph from the trunk)

Baseball stories brought out our father's unusual memory. He told the stories like they happened yesterday... Fendel Sitton was on first base and there were two out in the ninth... went details of a game. Here are a couple of baseball stories I recall. Cahone was most often the other team.

Players knew each other, even well. Just before the game was to begin Dad told the Cahone right fielder, jokingly yet knowing it might happen, he was going to "...Run your legs off today!" Dad threw right handed and batted left handed so his hits usually went to right field. (Everything he did with two hands, chopping wood, etc. was left-handed).

There weren't outfield fences around the fields, so a ball hit over a fielder or hard between fielders might roll a long way out. He hit three homeruns that day and Cahone's right fielder may have felt he was "running his legs off."

Of course, with many of Dad's baseball stories, his actions highlighted the play. The game was Rico playing a Montezuma Valley team. Dad played first base for Rico when he was older. It was the ninth inning and Rico needed one more out to win the game. The other team had a man on first who was threatening to steal second base. He was taking a long lead and with the next pitch the catcher threw the ball to Dad to put the tag on the runner. The runner made it back to first base safe. But Dad casually faked the throw back to the pitcher. The runner stepped off the base and Dad tagged him. The game was over—the old hidden ball trick!

Baseball games and dances were the entertainment events for the isolated communities. In homestead days Dove Creek did not have a theatre where people would gather, and so baseball, America's game, brought the communities together. I've heard about the Dove Creek team, the Cahone, Cortez, Dolores, Durango, Rico, Pleasant View and Telluride teams of the 1920s and 1930s. Even the sawmill town of McPhee had a team. The shape of Dolores County, Dad's employment, and the main population regions being located on east and went ends, enabled him to be a well-known player across the county, even in adjoining Montezuma County.

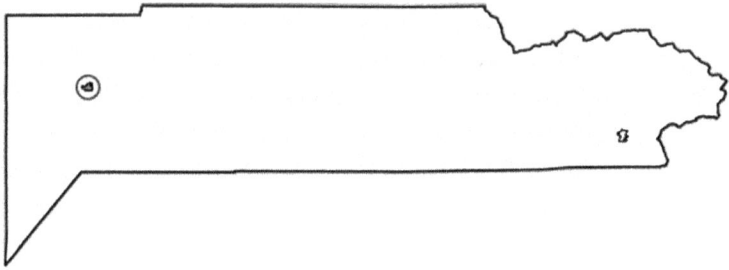

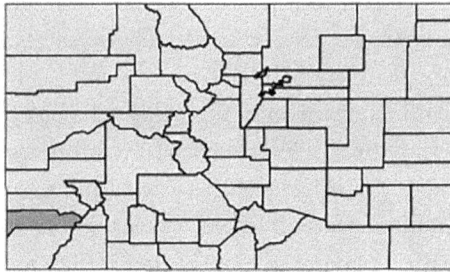

The upper figure shows the shape of Dolores County and the lower map shows its location in Colorado. The county only has two incorporated towns and they are about as far from each other as they can be and be in the same county. Rico is the old mining town and former county seat located in the eastern end of the county at 9,000 feet (right end of the upper figure). Dove Creek is in the western end of the county and only ten miles from San Juan County, Utah. Its elevation is 6,800 feet. The towns are 72 road miles apart. The county to the north is San Miguel County and to south is Montezuma County. (Maps by David Benbennick, public domain)

Until he was thirty-two, Dad played baseball for Dove Creek and against Rico. After that, he and his parents sold much of their homestead land and let farming go. They kept a small portion of the first homestead with the home where his parents lived. He began to keep full time employment in Rico while he played for the Rico Miners baseball team.

The economy of Rico was always unstable and depended upon the variables of the metals mining industry, mainly the price of the metals, and that depended on the demand. Rico flourished especially during war times. So, with the economy went the supply of baseball players and the successes of Rico's team. But for eight years with regular employment in the town, Dad was a mainstay of the Rico Miners team. And the team competed well with the teams to the south that were more stable with agriculture.

Cortez was the largest town in Montezuma County and had about 1,500 people in 1936. But in the Cortez region there were about 7,000 people, mostly farmers. By 1930 Montezuma County had several baseball teams. Durango was the largest town in southwestern Colorado in the 1920s and 30s and still is. Dad spoke of playing Durango once. The Durango game was when he played first base for the Montezuma-Dolores County All-stars late in his baseball playing life. Who won, what was the score? Other details I wish I knew. The Rico Miners of 1930, before the Great Depression hit Rico, were perhaps the best Rico town team he played for and were respected in the region. He spoke of players on that team. One he often mentioned was the shortstop, Studebaker, who he called Stude and I don't know his first name. I have a story of my own that goes with Stude.

In 1976 I attended my first national conference after becoming an Assistant Professor of Science Education at the University of Wyoming the year prior. The conference hosted a get together of the National Biology Teachers Association in Anaheim, California. We had nametags and at an evening dinner I sat across from a fellow about my age whose last name was Studebaker. I asked him where he was from and he named a California town, then said, "I'm originally from Colorado."

"Where in Colorado?" I asked.

"Telluride" he replied. "You probably haven't heard of it." (This was before Telluride became a famous ski town.)

"Oh yes I have," I said. "I was born in Rico." We had a link. Then I asked, "Did your dad go by Stude?"

"Yes," he said. I reached across the table and shook his hand.

"Stude and my dad played on the same Rico ball team." How many people were there in California in 1976? Only thirty-two million.

Dad loved his life in small town Rico where people knew each other and were friendly. He became acquainted with the happenings of the little mining town, its history, its stories and some that were well-known and repeated to newcomers about famous and distinguished residents. It was in 1982 Dad was asked by the Cortez librarian and Tommy Johnson, the newspaper reporter, to tell stories about his early days in Dolores County. He chose a story about two prominent Rico citizens when they were young men. It goes like this.

Charlie Engel Sr., who owned the Engel Mercantile in Rico, also owned mines. To make a public land mining claim become personal property, like with homesteads, the claimant needs to show he or she was preparing to mine or was carrying out mining for minerals. On Expectation Mountain, west of Rico, Charlie had a mine that needed to be worked to make Engel the owner. He hired two young men, or maybe they were just boys, but Rico natives, to go to the mine and carry out noticeable activity.

This story may have faded away early were it not for the fact that the young miners later became prominent residents of Rico. One was the young George Hicks who later became the superintendent of the Rico Argentine Mining Company and Dolores County Judge. He lived next door to us in Rico. The other was young Joe Koenig of the well-established Koenig family.

Near quitting time, Joe took a load of ore on a mine rail car to the entrance of the mine. George remained working back in the mine. At the entrance Joe saw a small water snake. For whatever reason, that Joe would have to explain, he wanted to take it home to Rico. How could he do that? There was the water sack hanging at the portal to the mine. He put the little snake in the water bag. (I've always wondered if he planned to use the sack again.) When George came to the entrance and needed a drink, he took but one. The snake went down his throat.

George said to Joe, "Something was in the water sack and it went down my throat."

"It was my snake," Joe answered, and they began the hurried trip to Rico, headed for the town's company doctor.

George told the doctor, "I swallowed a snake."

Dad or others who had heard the story could not name the Rico doctor that went with the snake event, but he gave George the remedy to throw up the snake. On tape, the snake story lives on in the annals of Dolores County history. Dad was asked to record pioneer times for the Cortez Library in 1982, a year before his death. Of all his stories, Dad gave the historians a vivid depiction of a moment in the day of the life of a guy from adjoining Dolores County.

After leaving Dove Creek farming, Dad continued living in Rico and worked at jobs he could find. The economy of Rico prior to the Great Depression was stable, mirroring the U.S economy. But it was baseball that was associated with Herald Keown. Now, living in Rico, he had other attributes the small county came to recognize, as well. People knew him for his caring and always helpful manners.

To live and stay in Rico, Dad needed permanent employment, and mills and mines didn't meet that need. The economy was always a roller coaster, ups and downs with the demand and price of metals. He never talked about the impetus to run for a Dolores County elective office, but he must have looked at the majestic courthouse, built in the golden years, and its elected occupants. The beautiful stone and brick building remains central to the small town. After becoming known to Rico and Dove Creek, and with the need for a continuing job, I'm sure for a while he had looked at that building and saw himself in one of its offices.

Though never the manager, he was the leader of the baseball team and that was important to Dove Creek and Rico. He played until 1936, when he was forty. It was hitting the baseball that made him known in the only two incorporated communities in Dolores County. Though he never revealed reservations or insecurities about his qualifications to handle the county's finances: debts, tax collection, foreclosures, the many duties of being a county treasurer, without doubt, there were plenty. To be the Dolores County Treasurer could be a job for all seasons.

At thirty-four he was elected County Treasurer. Several times he told me he was elected because he could "hit the ball." But we knew that was only one of many reasons. For thirteen years he was the treasurer and for his last two terms, eight years, he ran for the office unopposed.

It was 1930 when Dad was elected. I don't think he let it be known that he only had a tenth grade education. He said it was lucky for him to be a friend of Rowena Snyder who was the County Clerk. She knew his new position well and he often asked for help. But it was his position, and he sat behind the desk to carry out the duties of Dolores County Treasurer, beginning that first week in January of 1931.

Rowena Snyder (with Oral Lutener) was the Dolores County Clerk when Dad was elected County Treasurer In 1930. She knew the duties of Treasurer and was Dad's willing helper the first years of his thirteen years in the office. Oral Lutener was her assistant, who she later married. (Photograph from The Rio Grande Southern Story, Volume 5)

From January 1931 until the spring of 1944 Herald Keown was the Dolores County Treasurer. It was a daring adventure to run for the office and a very steep hill to climb that first year. The County Clerk, Rowena Snyder, knew his duties and he never quit thanking her for helping him survive in his first term. For more than thirteen years he was the Treasurer and was reelected without an opponent his last two terms (eight years). He resigned the position in 1944 when the position as Secretary and Treasurer for the Montezuma Valley Irrigation Company in Cortez, Colorado, opened. There was only a grade school in Rico. In 1946 the county seat for Dolores County was moved to Dove Creek. (Photograph from the trunk)

January 1931 was not a good time to learn about collecting taxes. The U.S. was into the Great Depression and times would only get worse. Dove Creekers struggled to pay property taxes even before the depression, but with agriculture crops going for give-away prices in the depression, collecting taxes for county treasurers across the country was not an enviable job.

In Dolores County, Dad by law was to announce, "Sheriff's Sales" of properties with unpaid taxes. He made the announcements in the Dolores Star, in Montezuma County. It was the newspaper nearest to Rico. Announcements went to the Montezuma Valley Journal, and the Cortez Sentinel, published in Cortez in Montezuma County. In earlier times Rico had newspapers but during the depression, Dolores County did not have a newspaper. The Dove Creek Press was first published in 1940. Some announcements of Sheriff Sales of properties because of unpaid taxes were for lands of people Dad knew, even friends.

Property tax payments beginning in 1931 became so difficult for Dolores County taxpayers that the County Treasurer did not take in enough revenue to have money to pay regular employees. My mother was one of those employees. She was teaching at the Peel School, northwest of Dove Creek. All Dad could do was send employees "I owe you" notes (warrants) for unpaid wages. These were warrants that went with a note to say Dolores County would pay you when enough tax revenues became available to cash the "I owe you." It was Dad's responsibility to notify those owed salaries when there was enough money in the county accounts to cash the warrants.

To talk with folks who lived through the Great Depression and hear of real experiences is enlightening when you realize the dire straits many folks experienced. In Chapter 7, Mom, in the one room Peel School, describes effects of extreme poverty for her students.

Rico in 1932 shows the effect of the Great Depression. There are few cars on the streets. The large building in the foreground is the Rico School. It was built in 1892. (Photograph from *The Rio Grande Southern Story*, Volume 5)

The public was highly nervous and extremely susceptible to rumors of impending financial disasters as banks closed. It was the Dolores County Treasurer who was responsible to invest and keep the county's tax revenues safe. Most of the funds were in the J.J. Harris & Company Bank down the river in Dolores. He never told me where he heard the rumor, but it did not turn out to be just a rumor. The J.J. Harris & Company Bank was about to close. He headed down the river on the dirt road in his DeSoto car and took all the money from the taxpayers from the bank. Its banking operations were suspended soon after.

J. J. Harris Bank in Dolores was the oldest bank in the Montezuma Valley and had its beginning in the first town of the Valley, Big Bend, two miles down river, southwest of Dolores. In 1891 the Rio Grande Southern Railroad entered the Dolores River Canyon two miles northeast of Big Bend and was going north to be connected to the mining towns of Rico and Telluride. The new railroad went north up the Dolores River, two miles northeast of Big Bend. The bank was moved to where the action would be. But in the Great Depression the oldest bank closed as well. (Source of photograph unknown)

On March 4, 1933 a "holiday for banks" was declared by the Colorado governor, Edwin C. Johnson. It was for all banks across Colorado and lasted until March 8.

The U.S. Secretary of Treasury called for "Holidays for banks," and holidays were to halt withdrawals and give banks a breather and hope some might accumulate funds to survive. More than 13,500 banks with deposits of nearly eight billion dollars suspended operations on account of financial difficulties that ended in 1933. There were no attorneys in the whole of Dolores County during Dad's tenure as Treasurer. In this role, Dad had dealings with well-known attorneys in both Cortez and Dolores, Dan Milenski and Jim Garrison. Both attorneys and Dad knew movement of the Dolores County seat to Dove Creek was imminent. Farming changed in the west end of Dolores County where the Thomas Keown family had homesteaded, and some farmers were becoming prosperous with raising pinto beans. But by the late 1930s, both of Dad's parents had passed on and he and Urban had sold the homesteads. In anticipation of the need of their children's education and greater opportunities ahead of them, Mom and Dad would need to leave Rico.

How successful was Herald Keown at being the Dolores County treasurer? The attorney, Jim Garrison, was a prominent and highly respected Montezuma County attorney and worked for Dolores County as well. In 1942 Dad and Mom decided it was time to move the family where there was a high school and more opportunities. He would not be a candidate for the 1944 election. In November of 1942 Dad asked Jim Garrison to write him a letter of recommendation for other employment. This is the letter.

In the spring of 1944, Herald Keown became the new Secretary and Treasurer for the Montezuma Valley Irrigation Company (MVIC) in Cortez. The water shareowners own the company that supplies water to farms of Montezuma Valley. He served in that position for 27 years until he retired in 1971, at age seventy-five.

JAMES B. GARRISON
Attorney at Law
DOLORES, COLORADO

November 28, 1942.

To Whom it may Concern:

Mr. H.G. Keown, the Former County Treasurer of Dolores County, Colorado at Rico, Colorado has asked that I write him a letter of recommendation. I am honored that he should make this favor of me, and gladly make the following statements concerning him and his ability.

I have known Mr. Keown since April of 1937. This been no passive acquaintance. My business has required that I become intimately acquainted with him and the conduct of his office which he voluntarily leaves at the end of this year.

Mr. Keown is a man who, in my judgment, embodies the sterling qualities that few men in public office ever have. I am irrevocably convinced of his honesty and integrity. His splendid record as County Treasurer and ex-officio Public Trustee of Dolores County speaks for itself. His tax collections rose to one of the highest in the State, his books and records were never adversely questioned upon audit; and yet, with all this, his personal popularity among the people of Dolores County has grown.

Mr. Keown is easy to get along with, and fits into any situation easily and speedily. He will stand up for what he honestly believes to be the right even in the face of considerable opposition and pressure. He is slow to form opinions, yet when formed, I have found they are usually correct.

Mr. Keown is a good diligent worker. He is conscientious and exacting. His knowledge of financial matters and office routine should qualify him for any responsible position in any office. These things I know and firmly believe.

In conclusion, I can sincerely say that I have enjoyed all my contacts with Mr. Keown, and I feel that Dolores County especially, is losing a fine man whom they will have great difficulty in replacing in elective or public office. I honestly believe that Mr. Keown will succeed in any task he undertakes, and that consideration given him will not be without its rewards, and that confidence placed in him will not be misplaced. I will be pleased to answer any further inquiry that may be directed to me concerning Mr. Keown.

Yours very truly,

James B. Garrison

JBG:bm

In 1946 the Dolores County seat moved to Dove Creek. On March 29 of 1944, as he took over his new position with the irrigation company, the new Secretary and Treasurer was announced by the Montezuma Valley Journal, one of two Cortez newspapers. Fifty years later, March 29, 1994, in the column called "Remember when....", his first day on his new job was remembered.

Remember when . . .

(From our files of 50 years ago)

Herald Keown today began his duties as the new Secretary and Office Manager of the Montezuma Valley Irrigation Company. He was formerly the county treasurer of Dolores County at Rico for many years, serving a number of terms of office after he had tried to resign and refused to let his name go on the ballot. This rather unusual situation came about when other candidates put on the ticket were elected but failed to qualify for the office. He is well-known throughout Southwestern Colorado, having lived in the vicinity of Dove Creek prior to entering politics in the neighboring county and is universally liked. His family will remain in Rico until the close of the school term when they expect to move to Cortez, if they can find a home.

The last phrase, "if they can find a home," was a sign of the time. World War II occupied the nation and all housing in Cortez, including the few motels, were occupied by Consciousness Objectors to the war. These men were building the Jackson Gulch Reservoir above the very small town of Mancos, seventeen miles east of Cortez. The reservoir would supply water through a pipeline to Mesa Verde National Park. Before the reservoir, much of the potable water for the park headquarters was collected rainwater on about two acres of tilted corrugated steel sheets. The system depended on unreliable rains. For other uses, and certainly not drinking, a deep-water well produced water that was so mineralized it would kill plants. Additionally, before the reservoir, potable water was hauled from Mancos.

For the new family in Cortez, housing would be a two-year challenge.

5

THE GAGES GO WEST

For John Gage, farming in Oregon County Missouri was not easy nor was it very profitable, but his family of eight were sustaining themselves in 1923. The money crop was cotton, a family enterprise that went with living on a farm that provided most of the food for the family. In that year the youngest son, Fay, who was eight years old, became afflicted with rheumatic fever (RF).

Before penicillin, rheumatic fever (streptococcal pharyngitis) had a high mortality rate. In fact, in the 1920s, rheumatic fever was the leading cause of death for those between five and twenty years of age. RF was the second leading cause of death, behind tuberculosis, for those twenty to thirty. The only treatments were salicylates (salts of salicylic acid) and bed rest. When doctors prescribed bed rest, victims usually remained home for weeks and the sickest of the children were sent to special institutions because it was thought to be very communicable.

In the 1920s there was not a specific diagnostic tool or symptomatic procedure accurate for recognition of RF. But Fay had the symptoms that today cause a specific diagnosis of RF. In recent times echocardiography, the use of echoes of the heart beating, is the surest way for physicians to diagnosis RF. But at that early age, Fay had developed a heart arrhythmia, an irregular heartbeat that was with him throughout his life.

Rheumatic fever is not spread from person to person as was believed in 1920. After 1942 came the experimental drug, penicillin, and RF today is treated with great success. But in 1920 the doctors of Oregon County Missouri told John and Mother Effie Gage that Fay should be in an arid climate where his life would not be cut short. John bought a used Model T Ford farm truck and the family prepared for the long trip to Bug Point, southwest of Dove Creek, Colorado.

A 1917 Model T Ford farm truck, similar to the one that in 1923 hauled the Gages from Thayer, Missouri to Bug Point, southwest of Dove Creek, Colorado, 1260 miles. The author's cousins, Norman Gage and Wayne Cook, do not agree about the tires. Wayne's mom, Edith, was riding with the other children in the bed of the truck. Wayne says Edith saw a balloon coming from a tire. It was a tube protruding from a break in a tire, not an uncommon event with the early pneumatic tires. Norman said his dad, Fay, told him the tires were hard rubber. The truck did not have a top over the cab. It had side boards and they had a tarp to put over the bed of the truck to cover the children and family belongings during rainy days. (Photograph from mtfca.com)

John Gage was aware of a neighbor who had homesteaded in the Dove Creek country and was planning to return to Oregon County, Missouri. His homestead was in an area called Bug Point. Grandpa traded one of his two Missouri farms for half of the homestead at Bug Point, eighty acres. The trade for the farm at Bug Point was sight unseen. With Mother Effie, the six children and their belongings, they boarded the truck and left Missouri in the middle of October, never to return as a family.

There were no plans to spend nights anywhere specific, but to camp along the way. In those years few travelers were booking motels. Certainly, the Gages did not have money for motels, even if motels were located routinely along the route.

Gage children are in this old and worn school picture. It was taken just before the Gage family left for Dove Creek, Colorado. John and Effie's children are identified. Bernice, age twelve is left most in the top row. Brian is eighteen and the tallest in the top row. Edith is sixteen and second from right in the top row. Lura was ten and is in the second row, third from left. Albia (Albie) was fourteen and is third from right in the second row, and Fay was eight and is in the front row, second from right. (Photograph from the trunk)

Using highway maps of 1920, the most likely route to Dove Creek from Thayer, Missouri, would have been to follow the main highways of that time and head due west. So, from the small town of Thayer the route was west to Poplar Bluff, Missouri, on to Williamsville, Willow Springs and through Springfield, Missouri. Then it was on to Joplin, into Kansas and toward Wichita. But before reaching Wichita they would have followed the Arkansas River west and gone through the farming towns along the river.

At that time, traveling to southern Colorado would have been following the Arkansas River to Pueblo. From Pueblo they went south on what is now Interstate 25 to Walsenburg and continued west again over La Veta Pass, elevation 9,413 feet, and into the San Luis Valley. In 1920 it was a dirt road over the pass, as were nearly all of Colorado pass roads at that time. From Walsenburg, my knowledge of the path to Dove Creek is more certain. Onward west from the San Luis Valley, except for the most adventuresome who would undertake Wolf Creek Pass in 1920, required a swing to the south into New

Mexico. This route would cross the most rugged Colorado range of mountains, the San Juans.

As described in the first chapter, towns of the San Luis Valley are atop an old dry lakebed, Lake Alamosa; even older than the Ice Age. The Valley is flat for a hundred miles north to south and seventy miles across, east to west. The Valley is a deceiving look at the topography of southern Colorado, and especially southwestern Colorado. For the last sixty years the regular route over the San Juans has been Wolf Creek Pass. My cousin, Max Houck, believes that was the Gage path in 1923. But his mom, Lura, said they were in New Mexico when they were approached by Indians and asked if they had whiskey to sell. These Indians were probably Navajos or Utes, both of which had reservations near Chama, New Mexico, where the Gages turned north. Drinking alcohol or sales of alcohol on either reservation was not allowed, nor were Native Americans allowed to buy alcohol off of the reservations.

Going over Cumbres Pass and to Chama would only have happened if the Gages went southwest to Antonito, Colorado, over the pass, and turned north at Chama to get back on the direct route to Dove Creek. Cumbres Pass was the safe path over the San Juan Mountains in 1920. Let me show the choice between Wolf Creek Pass that had only been open for seven years in 1923.

The Gages had a choice in crossing the San Juans, which wasn't a choice at all considering their six children and all of their belongings were in the back of the old truck.

Going over Cumbres Pass they crossed the Continental Divide and arrived at Chama, New Mexico. From Chama, the Gage's path was north to Pagosa Springs, Colorado. then, due west to Durango on Highway 160. Highway 160 was not designated as such until 1930.

When the Gages camped at night, sometimes it was near a town that maintained a campsite for travelers. A story told to me by my cousin Norman, shows the independence Grandpa Gage sought for his family, even in times when some fathers would have been asking for help. Many occasions in the hardship times of his life this independence surfaced.

Near a town camping area, the family put down their bedding and needed water for dinner and for the next day. Grandpa sent Fay and his older brother, Albie, to the nearby camping area for water. They were gone longer than expected and when they returned they told Grandpa the reason for their delay. They had accepted the invitation for dinner from another camping family along their trek for water. No handouts! It angered their dad and he let them know about the family's independence, notwithstanding the hard time they were experiencing.

A typical bend of the many sharp bends when Wolf Creek Pass was open to traffic in 1916. The elevation at the summit is 10,867 feet. The maximum grade is 7%. Sixty years later it still had a notorious reputation when C.W. McCall wrote the song, "Wolf Creek Pass." It became popular and established McCall as a writer of Colorado Rocky Mountain pass songs. Remember it? "Me an Earl was haulin chickens on a flatbed out of Wiggins, and we'd spent all night on the uphill side of thirty-seven miles of hell called Wolf Creek Pass. Which is up on the Great Divide." (Courtesy Photos)

A recent photograph near the summit of Cumbres Pass that goes between Antonito, Colorado and Chama, New Mexico. The summit is 10,022 feet and the maximum grade is 5.8%. (Photograph from tripadvisor.com)

For the children especially, not realizing the distance, the trip grew old. Sleeping on the ground, the food and the preparation of the food without a kitchen, or even the security of water and toilets were testing their patience. Cousin Norm said the trip took most of a month. My dad said more than two weeks. Most cousins knew of a breakdown on the way when a wheel had to be replaced. Where along the way the wheel went out, and how long the wait was for a replacement, we do not know.

Durango was the largest town in the southwest region of Colorado and headquarters for federal services, especially the San Juan Mining District. In 1923 Durango's population was 4,100.

Durango, Colorado about 1920. (Photograph from Legendofamericas.com)

From Durango it was forty-eight miles farther west to Cortez, the largest town and county seat of Montezuma County, Colorado, and fifty-two miles from the Bug Point destination. In 1920 Cortez's population was only 600, but it had a high school. The farms around Cortez were productive with irrigation water from the Montezuma Valley Irrigation Company, developed around 1900. The water-user-owned company took water from the Dolores River, twelve miles to the north of Cortez and sent it through a mile long tunnel. The tunnel had been installed shortly after Cortez was founded. It went through the south Dolores River canyon wall and the Valley was irrigated. But the irrigation system only watered farms about twelve miles north of Cortez, twelve miles west, ten miles south and five miles east of Cortez. The land west, beyond the irrigated farms, was known as the "dry land" and that is where the Gages were headed. Bug Point was another fifty miles to the southwest corner of Dolores County and Colorado, beyond the community of Dove Creek. It was arid, like the Oregon County doctors had prescribed for Fay. Annual precipitation for Dove Creek is 14.8 inches. Where they came from in Oregon County, Missouri, the annual precipitation is 47 inches.

Finally, thirty-five miles west of Cortez, the Gages came to Dove Creek. In 1920 the road through Dove Creek was dirt and it would remain dirt for at least another fifteen years before it became gravel. There was only one mercantile store, the Parley Butts Mercantile, that was only nine years old in 1923. The whole town consisted of a few buildings built near a small ephemeral creek called Dove Creek. It was named for the common mourning dove of the pinion-juniper forest that grows mostly in draws of the region. Vegetation grows best in the area from wind-blown soil from the southern desert and is red-brown. On ridges and rims the soil forms in place from the bedrock that is the Dakota Sandstone. It is clay-rich yellow-gray sandstone. It often outcrops and runs a hundred miles east to west. It is the bedrock for most Dolores and Montezuma County towns and is less covered with soil as it tapers south to the dry Navajo Reservation.

Our family joked about Grandpa Gage's first stop and orientation in Dove Creek as he looked for directions to Bug Point. He wasn't much for using maps, and most likely there wasn't a map with Bug Point on it. But his way of locating his destination was to ask a person in the vicinity of his terminus. He would usually ask the stranger, "Do you know where so and so lives?" We imagine him stepping into the Parley Butts Mercantile with the question, "How do I get to Bug Point?" To find out where Bug Point was from Dove Creek, knowing the condition of roads, and the fact that so few people lived several miles southwest of Dove Creek, must have caused both the storekeeper and Grandpa some bewilderment. Bug Point was still seventeen miles away and the road to the farm and only house at Bug Point, the one they acquired in the trade, might be another half day at their speed. How should they be prepared for a stay there?

They knew there wasn't water on the farm, and it would need to be hauled. For water at Bug Point, it was the seventeen miles back to Dove Creek and the well at the Parley Butt's store. The water they took from Dove Creek was in wooden barrels and would be used very sparingly. The family's existence for nearly a year at Bug Point was with many questions and to all of the cousins, unanswered. Would they have relied on Butt's store for food? For that pioneering trip to Bug Point, food was probably purchased in Cortez. There was only one house at Bug Point, and it was theirs. And one hundred years later, last summer, when we arrived at the house, it was still the only house. If it had been lived in since the Gages lived there it does not have that appearance. The nearest house is a home about a mile east that has been built in recent years.

The old house still standing at Bug Point, seventeen miles southwest of Dove Creek, Colorado. It was the first home in Colorado for the Gage family of eight. They traveled in an old farm truck 1,260 miles from their Thayer, Missouri cotton farm. They arrived at this, their new home, on Halloween, 1923. (Photograph by Joy Keown, August 2019.)

Cousin Norm, son of Fay, seems to have gained the most complete story of Bug Point from his dad. Also, it was his association in his youth with Grandpa and Grandma Gage. Fay's family lived for a while with Grandpa on the Gage farm five miles west from Dove Creek; the farm we all knew. Fay helped Grandpa farm the place and build the barn that was new when we were kids.

Grandpa Gage homesteaded the farm we came to call Grandpa and Grandma's farm. Actually, they took over a homestead and the expected development requirements to claim the homestead land. That was in 1924, after less than one year at Bug Point. Money from the sale of the second Missouri farm was used to purchase equipment to farm.

6

DRY LAND FARMER AND PROHIBITION SHERIFF

In so many ways, to know Granddad Gage was to know my mother. The knock on the door that Saturday morning was Grandpa Gage. "I believe they're going to make five sacks to the acre, Bernie," he said to my mom that morning before he said hello and stepped in the door. It was another laugh we had about our Grandpa Gage's enthusiasm for farming.

Five sacks per acre for pinto beans was a bumper dry land crop. Those are one hundred pound sacks of beans that in 1949 went for about eight dollars per 100-pound bag. That year Grandpa had about 200 acres of beans or $8,000 worth of pinto beans. He sold them and went to Durango, Colorado and bought a new 1949 Packard sedan—cash. The last vehicle he had driven other than tractors was the pre 1920 truck that he used to move the family from Thayer, Missouri in 1923. His new Packard in 1949 cost about $4,000. Never had farming been more than a get by living for Grandpa, and often not even that. But he loved it. He was a farmer through and through.

Grandpa's 1949 Packard Sedan looked much like this one. His was an army green color. (Photograph from classics.com.free photos)

Riding with Grandpa in his 49 Packard was an exciting experience. If the speed limit was 60 miles per hour, he drove 65. If there were curves in the road, that brought on the excitement. He would keep that speed of 65 and then hit the brakes like they were hairpin curves. Pity us (no safety belts in those days) and the car behind. Then, he was quickly back to just above the speed limit.

Before farming pinto beans around World War II time, though farming was his passion, it had not been good to him. But his family saw him through the low times. His farming during his younger midlife years was a family affair, and helpful neighbors were important to his farming survival. In Missouri the family picked cotton together. In Colorado, from my own observation, his sons and neighbors kept his equipment functioning and carried out other necessary chores that went with success at farming. And when crops were complete failures and he didn't have money to sustain the family through winters, the whole family would pitch in. One fall in the 1920s the family went to Montezuma Valley to pick an apple crop for an apple farmer named Brumbaugh.

Brumbaugh turned out to be lacking scruples or empathy for the Gages' condition. They went to the Valley to secure money to make it through the winter. Grandpa contracted for the family to pick the apple crop for an agreed price. It was school time and instead of being in school, Grandpa's school-age children were picking apples.

Mother told few stories, but she told the Brumbaugh story with zest. The family picked the apple crop and the children were well aware of the terms of the agreement to harvest the crop. But Brumbaugh would not carry out the accord and wanted to pay the Gages much less than the agreement called for. Whether it was a signed paper agreement, I don't know. Our grandfather would not take what Brumbaugh offered. But instead, having been a deputy sheriff in Missouri, he was familiar with the court system that could help his family recover the money owed them. He filed a case in the Montezuma County Court and soon the entire family sat in the courtroom as claimants against Brumbaugh.

Mother was called to the witness stand knowing well the terms of the contract. She said she was really nervous about being a witness until she heard Brumbaugh's defense of his shortchanging the family, and he was not honest. She said, "Then I wasn't nervous at all. I told the judge that our family carried out the agreement and Brumbaugh was not being honest." The Gages won and Brumbaugh paid in full.

For the Gages, they had always endured as a family and to understand their closeness one would need to have experienced the brothers' and sisters' lives as adults, when they were miles apart. Other than short weekend picnics up the Dolores River or into the La Plata Mountains, we only took one family vacation. It was in the summer of 1953. It was not to Yellowstone, or Disneyland, or to see any of the big American vacation draws. It was to see Mother's brothers and sisters who were pulled apart for employment by the Great Depression. Three of her siblings lived in California. Only my mother and younger brother, Fay, remained in the home range; Fay in Monticello, Utah and our family in Cortez. The Gages would never let the family togetherness go. A testimony to the affection that always occurred when the oldest Gage brother, Bryan, was leaving to return to Prague, Oklahoma, forty miles from Oklahoma City.

Bryan left Dove Creek at the time of the depression and was employed by an airplane factory from the time of World War II until he retired in the 60s. He went up the ladder and always drove a new car. Pontiacs were his favorite. Materialism was his weakness and it outcropped in his conversations with us. It was things, and more things. But when Bryan was saying goodbye, ready to drive nonstop to Prague, when he hugged my mom he always broke into tears.

The aging, but smiling, Gage siblings are together at the Keown home in 1979. Smiling is expected for photos but when the brothers and sisters of this very close family were together, smiles just happened. Edith (Cook) Gage is left, then Fay Gage, Lura (Houck) Gage, Albia Gage, Bernice (Keown) Gage and Bryan Gage. (Photograph from Keown family photos)

I often ask, what kept the Gages so together, though they were so far apart? Was it the courage and unity they felt in facing the impediments to their family's survival? Was it the knowledge learned as they saw that each was vulnerable without the others? They learned that togetherness was a successful strategy and saw each member as vital to the whole. In 1923 they were going with their parents to a land unknown so their young brother would be healthy. It worked. Fay became healthy and they would sacrifice other times when the team, the united family, was called upon again.

There was no employment for her brothers, and their dad became the Dolores County Sheriff for a regular job and income, though times were so bad he didn't have a car. Mother had a job and sent money from her meager teaching wages to help the family through the depths of the depression era. As they stayed bonded through their struggles, there developed that ill-defined feeling and awareness of love.

And what about the oldest daughter, Edith? From my cousins, it has been difficult to learn where she was in the Gage story. Grandpa saw her as a sincere partner in farming. The production of the garden in that dry land county was like the money crop, dependent on rain.

Edith worked the garden and her sincere interest in the farm carried over to the small family farm near Durham, California where she lived most of her adult life. From her daughter Carol (Tookie we call her), I heard that Edith was the small farm manager. She could do all of the duties: raise chickens, livestock, grow a garden and flowers, and at the same time be the kind and loving mother of six children. It was important to her to see that her children were educated, and they were.

There were other hard times while the children of Grandpa and Grandma Gage lived at home, instances when Grandpa had to act in desperation for his family. One of those times, in the 20s, before pinto beans had become the money crop of profit—and for some, even wealth, Grandpa planted about fifty acres of potatoes. He was sure they would do well in the level watershed draw of the farm where moisture exceeded that on land higher on hills and the slopes. In Montezuma Valley and with dry land neighbors, Grandpa knew there would be a reliable market for his potatoes. I am familiar with the land where Grandpa planted the potatoes. As a teenager, I hoed weeds and stacked pinto beans in the same acreage. And boy did those potatoes grow!

In mid-summer the plants were large and there was promise and excitement for a great potato harvest. But before the plants made potatoes, an early freeze came and killed every last one of them. Mother said Grandpa was literally sick. He packed his bag, took a bus, then a train, and headed to

California. He packed lettuce that winter and sent money home until it was time in the spring to farm again.

In the late 1920s, farming the Dove Creek land was a gamble at best. It was the time when my dad headed for the San Juan mines and mills to supplement the meager income that farming the homesteads produced. The same year, 1930, when Dad was elected Dolores County Treasurer, Grandpa Gage decided to use his Missouri deputy sheriff experience and run for Dolores County Sheriff. I know he had other skills, but he wasn't a natural politician. Yet with his eight years near Dove Creek, he was probably best known for his endurance; and like my mother, he had tenacity and resoluteness. But he was also known for his physicality: barrel-chested, about one hundred and eighty pounds, and soft spoken. One time he told me that at county fairs in Missouri they always had a hundred yard dash. Casually he said, "I always won." My Dad said that once behind Parley Butt's Mercantile he "cleaned up" on a guy who insulted him. The guy was one of the tough, roughshod fellows who was among a hard brand from the area. Some were there to make whiskey and were located in the isolated canyons. But they got to Dove Creek for needed supplies. Whether Grandpa's combatant was a bootlegger, I don't know. He was not one of the community-spirited sorts who sustained the difficult lives of homesteaders. Word spread, but not through the bush. Most of the bush had been grubbed out by 1930.

Besides being good with his fists, Granddad's well-known principles were recognized in the Dove Creek country. He was a family man who had the spirit and endurance for those hard times. He was elected and in January 1931, like my dad who was elected County Treasurer and living in Rico, began serving his first term as Dolores County Sheriff. He had just turned fifty years old. I will add, he didn't have a car. That fact is difficult to fathom today. The Great Depression had set in and the county was so poor it could not buy the sheriff a car. He was dependent upon willing neighbors with autos to carry out his duties. The jail and the sheriff's office were in Rico, 76 miles away from Grandpa's home. Grandpa's home had become his office. But if he had a prisoner who was due jail time, an agreement with Montezuma County required a 35 mile drive by Grandpa with his prisoner to the jail in Cortez; in a neighbor's car who was paid for the trip by Dolores County.

Prohibition of the sale and manufacture of alcohol beverages began in 1920 and ended in 1933. By Grandpa's first term, illegal whiskey-making was rampant in the Dove Creek country. Though it was illegal by the U.S. Constitution (Amendment 18) to make and to sell whiskey, it was not illegal to drink it, and the market for bootleg whiskey was well established. The sparsely populated Dolores County, with its isolated canyons, was seen by moonshiners as the ideal place to distill whiskey. It was usually made from corn.

As discussed briefly in Chapter 1, before Prohibition, the 18th Amendment to the Constitution established the prohibition of "intoxicating liquors" in the United States. It was first known as the Volstead Act and it went into effect on December 5, 1920. But before being repealed in 1933 with Amendment 21, it became known as "The Law of Unintended Consequences."

It eventually led to Al Capone and the mafia. By 1931 when Grandpa Gage took office as Dolores County Sheriff, prohibition had become very unpopular among a large portion of Americans and was especially difficult to enforce. Enforcement was the responsibility of Federal Agents and it was intended that the agents would get cooperation from local law enforcement officials, such as police departments and county sheriffs. But the cooperation by local law officials was generally almost non-existent. For a while in New York, the New York Police Department officers were told by the chief and mayor not to work with the federal agents at all—"they have too many more important law-enforcement duties to do."

Prohibition was meant to clean up crime in the country, but crime increased. The closing of large breweries and saloons not only put thousands out of work, but the very large share of taxes these enterprises paid to the federal government ceased, crippling the abilities of the U.S. government to carry out expected projects and functions.

But the most important negative result of Prohibition was that the production of drinking alcohol went underground. Actually, it wasn't even underground. A regular supply of moonshine whiskey was consistently delivered to some members of the U.S. Congress at their offices. Many citizens knew who was making the bootleg whiskey and where it was being made. And since the 18th Amendment didn't forbid drinking the spirits, most who really wanted a drink knew where to get it. And other than ignoring this act of Congress and the state legislatures, they remained law-abiding citizen. However, Prohibition in the long run caused less respect for government and its regulations. And often it wasn't good whiskey bootleggers sold. It has been estimated that during Prohibition one thousand Americans died each year from drinking "bad booze."

Such was the state of the nation's Prohibition when Grandpa Gage became the county sheriff. Actually, it was nearing the end of the "noble experiment," as it came to be called. A main reason it was so difficult to enforce was that many local law officers failed to cooperate with the Federal Agents, the Revenuers, and took bribes from bootleggers to conceal their business. The illegal whiskey and beer makers paid police, sheriffs, and county and district attorneys to look the other way.

How would the enforcement of the ban affect a new county sheriff in a hot spot for bootleggers and makers of the illegal moonshine? Most men and women who were making illegal booze viewed the prohibition of their occupation as an infringement on freedom and a way in hard times to make a living. Federal Agents came from Durango and their expectation was that the Dolores County Sheriff would know where the illegal distilleries were located. And they were right. Grandpa did know most of the moonshiners, though he himself was a teetotaler. That fact and his principles were reasons why he was elected. And knowing Grandpa, he would be the last law officer to take a bribe from a whiskey maker in order to keep him hidden.

With the agents, Grandpa led the enforcers to several stills and helped to destroy them and arrest the owners. His kids were at home in his early tenure as sheriff and one summer night they smelled smoke. "The house is on fire!" What a call it must have been to know the bootleggers would destroy what little the family had and would even take their lives. Grandpa opened the door and the south side of the house was spewing flames. As he opened the front door, there was a gunshot and a bullet hit the facing on the door on his right side. He ran to the cistern for water to put out the fire. The arsonist was close by and ran through the yard. In the darkness he caught his head on the clothesline. He kept running but lost his hat. Grandpa put out the fire and collected the hat.

Grandpa was nearly a one-man Dolores County law enforcement agency. The only incorporated towns were Dove Creek and Rico and they had marshals. There were no detectives or under sheriffs, or other law officials to call on. Like other sheriffs, he probably saw busting stills and arresting moonshiners as the Feds job, but he and the family were getting the consequences, the revenge of moonshiners. It was serious danger. With other Dove Creekers, he tried to connect the hat with its owner but wasn't able to do so. The arsonist and the shooter who put the bullet in the door facing, only two feet from his head, were never arrested. Until the house and farm was sold and the original house remodeled, we saw the bullet hole every time we entered the front door.

John Gage seemed to be baptized by fire in his first term as Dolores County Sheriff. Prohibition in making alcohol caused Grandpa nightmares. He had been the sheriff for only seven months when late in the afternoon of July 31, 1931, an argument broke out between Alfred Rittenhouse and Albert McGee in Jim Posey's store (originally the Parley Butt's Mercantile) in Dove Creek. It concerned crops and water. McGee had a well and he put a padlock on it to prevent "trespassers." Dove Creek did not have a newspaper at the time, but I have been able to gather considerable details from three old Cortez newspapers of the time, thanks to the Cortez Library's archives person, Sally Jo Leitner.

Rittenhouse and McGee owned adjoining farms in the Cedar Point region, not far from Dove Creek. There had been previous conflicts. Folks said there was "bad blood." McGee was older than Rittenhouse but for only what is now a supposed reason, McGee lunged at Rittenhouse. There was a witness, Mark Posey, who said that before the fight broke out he wasn't paying close attention. The younger Rittenhouse knocked McGee down. Then, Rittenhouse knocked him down again. But when McGee came up the second time he had a knife and he stabbed Rittenhouse in the left lung. It was the critical wound of several. Rittenhouse went out staggering to the front door when another witness named Sell caught Rittenhouse as he was falling and heard him say, "I did not call him a liar." The words were near his last, for within five minutes he was dead.

After killing Rittenhouse, McGee didn't flee the store. He waited for the county sheriff to arrive and was arrested. To make the arrest, a Dove Creek resident went for Sheriff Gage and when Grandpa arrived at the store he handcuffed McGee. But then he needed a Dove Creeker with a car to take McGee to the Cortez jail. By then it was late and that would not happen until the next morning. So Grandpa, with a neighbor to drive the car, took McGee to his home. Besides his wife, Effie, I don't know if children were home. Fay, the youngest at that time, would have been seventeen. Grandpa handcuffed McGee to his bed and sat there through the night with his 32-revolver in hand. He waited for the morning when a neighbor would drive the sheriff and his prisoner to the Cortez jail.

The trial of McGee began May 10, 1932, nearly a year after the murder, at the County Court House in Rico. It took longer to settle for a jury than it did to convict McGee. The trial lasted but one afternoon and a day. On May 11 the jury found McGee guilty of voluntary manslaughter. On June 15 the District Judge, J.M. O'Rourke, sentenced him to not less than four years, and not more than seven years, to the State Penitentiary. Why such a light sentence for voluntary murder? Rittenhouse wasn't an angel. He had spent time with partners in the Cortez jail for making moonshine whiskey in Montezuma County. He knocked the older man down twice at Posey's store and may have again. But a maximum of seven years for voluntary manslaughter? My mother said the Dove Creek community saw McGee as an angry sort. He carried a knife on his hip, and it wasn't because he was fond of whittling.

After completing a master's degree in biology at Colorado State University, I went to Monticello, Utah to teach sciences at the Monticello High School. I taught there for five years, went to Ball State University in Muncie, Indiana, and completed a doctorate in biology. But a much better paying position than being a professor somewhere was offered to me if I were to become the Junior High School Principal in Blanding, Utah. It was twenty-five miles south of Monticello and only about forty miles from Lockerby, a community in Colorado by the state line, and eight miles from Dove Creek. In late August, I went for my first haircut in Blanding. The barber was the only barber in Blanding, a town of about two thousand conservative Mormons.

The barber was an older fellow, friendly and probably glad for a new customer. He asked where I was from and I told him I was raised in Cortez. "Years ago," he said. "I used to get over to Colorado often to play at dances. It was when we had a dance band. I remember playing at Lockerby. It was the depression and prohibition days."

And then he went on about playing for community dances at Lockerby. He said, "There it wasn't affected by bootleggers like some places the band played. There was a sheriff who walked over from his home and sat there by himself on a bench through the whole dance. He just sat there, and everyone had a good time. There just wasn't anyone drunk or causing commotion."

Then I asked, "Do you know his name?"

"No, he said, "But everyone respected him and while he sat there, there just wasn't any trouble."

"Was his name John Gage?" I asked.

"Yes," he answered.

"He was my Granddad," I said. The two of us were surprised. I knew more about Grandpa's service as the county sheriff and his reputation. But the respect for him and observance of his presence by the Lockerby community really didn't surprise me. I will add that I have clocked the distance he may have walked to Lockerby from his farm. It is three miles. But I'm not sure he walked home in the wee hours of the morning. He didn't have a car in the thirties, but for carrying out other duties of the sheriff, friends and neighbors often gave him a lift.

The Lockerby Community Hall where folks gathered for all occasions, but especially to dance, stood at the top of this hill. Long since the Depression and Prohibition days dances, the hall was razed. (Photograph by Joy Keown, July 2019)

Our granddad ran for a third term as sheriff but was not elected. He still didn't have a car to drive, not a county car or his own. My dad said he probably couldn't get the job done. He was more of a farmer than a sheriff. His heart was always in farming. Being a sheriff was a supplement job when he really needed the money to be a dry land farmer. A family member with a regular job in the Depression in 1932 was my mother and she loaned money to her folks, brothers, and sisters. She was the teacher at Peel School northeast of her parent's home, and then a teacher at Coal Bed School, five miles from the Gage farm, during the school year 1933-34.

Grandpa Gage sits on his tractor about 1950. (Photograph from the trunk)

Another hardship on the Gage farm came in 1943 when the crop was pinto beans. It wasn't a complete crop failure, but Grandpa could see he and Grandma would not make it through until another crop would be sold the next summer. So again, Grandpa headed for California. But by that time there were no children at home and Grandma had become crippled. With two crutches she made her way to the outhouse. She was 63. He was criticized for leaving her. Uncle Fay lived in Monticello, Utah, 22 miles away and Mother was in Rico, 76 miles away. His other children were in Oklahoma and California. Even the closest neighbors at the time were not close. Grandma didn't have a phone, either. Actually, few farmers did. But again, it was because of his independence that Grandpa was reluctant to ask for help.

In California, Granddad used his sheriff experience to become a guard at Grayson Heat Control Systems, Inc. He needed to carry his 32-caliber pistol and was issued a California permit to do so.

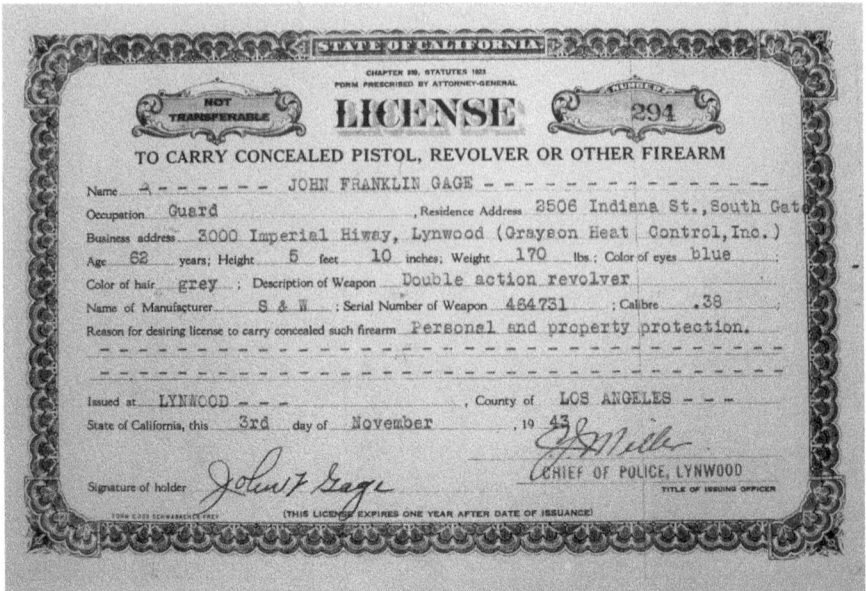

California license to John Gage to carry his concealed 32-caliber revolver pistol. (Photograph from the trunk)

The last story about our grandfather doesn't glorify him or put him on a pedestal, but it portrays him for his ways and how he was aging. The event took place when I was fourteen years old and grandpa was seventy.

Our granddad hired my cousins, Norman and David Gage, and myself to stack pinto beans in his fields. Stacking the beans came after they were cut and lying in rows. To thresh the bean plants and separate the plant from the beans, plants needed to be put into small piles in rows. Then the threshing machine would grab the pile and separate beans from the dried plant.

It was the summer of 1951, probably in late August and two years after Grandpa bought the new 1949 Packard. He used that Packard for all purposes on the farm. Being his first auto since owning the truck that moved the family in 1923, one would suppose he would give it special care, but he treated it like it was his farm truck. If it was ever washed during the four years he owned it, I would be surprised. It was traded for a new 1953 Packard.

There were red-brown dirt roads at the edges of the fields, and he drove on those roads until we reached our destination for the day and began the bean stacking. I don't remember whether the Packard had air conditioning, but probably not in 1949. That August morning as we drove the paved road to where we turned off to the red dirt road to his field, the windows were down. On the dirt road, dust would really come in and the windows went up. When the workday was over, after sitting all day in the sun, the Packard was hot. As we began the trip to the house, windows were down but as the dirt was sucked in, windows went up again. Grandpa chewed tobacco and a new chew went in his mouth as we started the trip back to his house. But after just a short distance down the road, Grandpa needed to spit tobacco and he did. But the tobacco spit went about eight inches and hit the closed window. Honestly, that is the only time I ever heard him swear. "Shit!" he said. We drove on. Whether he did at least a partial cleaning of his car and the window, I don't remember.

Our grandmother, Effie Gage, seriously suffered from rheumatism for many years, even before she became old. It seemed to us that the hardships of her life pulled her down in health and disposition to a much greater extent than they did for Grandpa. She was born Effie Barton in April 24, 1881 in Dallas County Missouri. She gave birth to seven children. The first, Basil, died early. He was named Basil after Grandpa's brother and best friend, Basil. Their closeness and friendship caused us to know Basil and his wife, Calma, better than most great uncles.

The brothers never let the miles keep them apart for long spaces of time. When Basil and Calma came to see Grandpa, time was spent at our home. Basil and Calma were an engaging couple and I remember them as being light-hearted. That is, until, Dad, Basil, and Grandpa—especially Basil and Dad—got into politics. The three of them were Republicans and in their conversations, Democrats caught hell.

Great Uncle Basil Gage and Grandpa Gage are at our Cortez home in about 1955. Like my dad, Basil was a World War I veteran and served in northern Siberia where the Army protected a large oil deposit from the Germans. Stories about his Siberian service fascinated us. (Photograph from the trunk)

My sisters and I don't remember Grandma Gage when she was not crippled. I remember when she began to walk with one crutch. Mother and my sisters went to Dove Creek and the farm, forty miles from Cortez, to help with the household chores that had become difficult for her. I accompanied Mom and my sisters a few times, but I don't remember doing housework; that's because I didn't do any. Long hours while Grandpa was in the fields, Grandma sat in her wicker chair where she could look out the north window and wait for Grandpa's return, often at dark when it was time to light the coal oil lantern.

I remember Grandpa was often short with words for Grandma. He was a man of few words, but even too few words with his wife. To be around them, and young as we were, there would be doubt about their love for each other, especially his affection for her. My doubts were abolished when I went to Grandma's funeral, my first funeral. It was an open casket funeral and at the end of the service, this man of few words, who was often too brief with Grandma, cried and cried as he leaned over her body. They had been through so much together.

That is the way it was at Grandpa and Grandma's farm. When it got dark, the kerosene (coal oil) lanterns were lit and it was a short time later before we were in bed. And the beds were not like ours in Cortez. They were feather mattresses and we sank into the comfort they offered.

Grandma Gage had passed away before the house got electricity, switch-on lights, and the conveniences that go with electricity. But she loved to garden and raise flowers, even on crutches. I always remember Grandma and Mom's Missouri lineage from a fact told to us by Mother. Mom's grandfather back in Missouri left home and joined the Union forces in the Civil War. He was only 14 and became a bugle boy. When my sister, Beverly, and I were into "the trunk" for family history, we found this photograph of Effie (Barton) Gage's parents, Mother's grandparents.

Grandma Gage died August 1, 1949 in Cortez. She was sixty-eight.

Mother and my sisters continued trips to Dove Creek to keep up the housework and check Granddad's stock of groceries, as Grandpa continued farming. We were always a one-car family, so Dad drove them to the farm, left them for two or three days, and picked them up come the weekend.

Robert and Mary Barton, Mom's grandparents. Robert joined the Civil War and was a bugle boy. (Photograph from the trunk)

In Cortez, I was deep into baseball during the summers and rarely stayed at the farm, but I remember one time I did stay. I remember that I couldn't bring my vaulting pole and high jumping pit that I had constructed behind our Cortez home. With junior high aged friends in the east end of Cortez, it was a popular attraction. So, at Grandpa's I proceeded to make a vaulting pole from a long and narrow piece of wood found near the barn. I fashioned it with my pocketknife. But of course, there was not a pit full of any landing material like the one in the backyard of my home. I had filled it with sawdust from the irrigation company's mill. So, at Grandpa's farm I vaulted without a pit and hoped for a feet down landing. Perhaps vaulting at the farm is well remembered because I vaulted over the clothesline, the same one that took off the arsonist's hat during Prohibition days. I did not realize, nor did friends in Cortez who vaulted at my pit, that vaulting poles were made of bamboo or aluminum for reasons other than lightness. They would not break like a pine pole might, and possibly become a spear.

Much of the time when I became well acquainted with our grandpa he was single and living on the farm by himself. He was in Oklahoma at his brother

Basil's home in the winter when he met a woman, Hallie, who's occupation was a house mother at a University of Oklahoma fraternity in Norman, Oklahoma. She was younger than Grandpa, but not by much. Their engagement was only a short time.

Hallie had the romantic idea that she could be a farmer's wife on an isolated southwestern Colorado farm, like a homesteader's wife. I hope she knew that the farm didn't have electricity, an indoor toilet (the outhouse was about forty yards from the house), and water was carried in buckets from a hand dug well to a cistern near the kitchen door. The well was at least a quarter of a mile away. She had not been to the farm when we met her in Cortez on their way to Dove Creek.

The romanticism of life on the homestead waned quickly. Soon the Rural Electric Association (REA) had a line to the home. An indoor toilet and bathtub were installed between a new bedroom addition on the south side of the house. A well was drilled close to the house, and hard well water from deep in the ground, with an electric pump, put water to the kitchen sink and bathroom. Everyone in Dove Creek, or near the town who had deep-water wells, had the very mineralized water. If a lawn was watered and it struck the house, an orange rainbow was left to identify where the hard water evaporates had landed.

Whether Hallie had ever used an outhouse, we don't know. Probably by the 1950s Grandpa had gone to toilet paper. We cousins remember when we first became acquainted with Grandpa and Grandma's outdoor toilet, the old Montgomery Ward catalog served for toilet paper. Our dad had an expression that went with the mail-order toilet paper. It was also a calendar. The expression came into being long before we kids were acquainted with the Gage outhouse. He would say, "It is late in the year. We're down to the harness section of the catalog."

Once on a trip to the outhouse my mother encountered a rattlesnake. She had a great respect for poisonous snakes, and disliked snakes of all kinds. She said that one time in Missouri while bringing the cows in to milk, she and Aunt Lura (Charlie was her nickname) came upon a rattlesnake, a copper head, and as they began to cross a stream, there was a water moccasin. Her fears came early. She was only twelve when they first lived at Bug Point, a good habitat for rattlesnakes, but not so good for invaders of their territory. We kids were always warned to look for rattlers on the route to the toilet.

For water at the Gage home, Hallie must have insisted early on that a well be dug near the house. The hand-dug well was a long way from the house. Mother talked about carrying water from the well to the cistern that was located near the kitchen door. From the cistern bucket, water went to the only sink in the house that was in the kitchen. But to get water to the cistern, it was a half-mile walk at least to the well and back, and the return trip was with a near-full bucket of water. It was a plainly learned family lesson to use water sparingly. Mom said she thought her right arm was longer than her left from carrying water from the well those many years.

The old well site today is at the hollow behind a broken pond dam that a later owner built. He knew there was ground water down about ten feet and he dug a hollow with a Caterpillar to it. Cattails now grow in the hollow. (Photograph by Joy Keown, July 2019)

But the comforts Hallie added were not enough. The great differences of her city life in Norman, Oklahoma and the isolated and lonely life on the farm, with her husband's days in the fields, were beyond her romantic expectations of life in the west.

The marriage did not last long, about two years, and Hallie went back to Oklahoma. Grandpa was living alone again with the conveniences that we called the "after-Hallie" add-ons. He was farming his farm and living in a house that was much more modern.

Gage's farmhouse has been added to and remodeled several times since Grandpa died and Wilmer and Lorena Dickens bought the farm. This photograph was taken in the summer of 2019. The door where Grandpa was shot at by bootleggers is beneath the overhang at the right in the photograph, on the east side, the front of the home. The whole south end of the home we call "Hallie's addition." The original cistern is still in use under the overhang on the backside (left side in the photograph) of the house. (Photograph by Joy Keown, July 2019)

The story of our granddad's later years of farming would be incomplete without telling about his son, Fay, and the wonderful neighbors, the Dickens, less than a quarter of a mile away.

For the first years of his marriage, Fay's family lived on a farm that came to his family through his marriage to Barbara Johnson of Monticello. The large wheat and pinto bean farm was at Horsehead, a farming region in Utah, just across the state line about ten miles from the family farm at Dove Creek. Fay and his family were good to Grandpa. Granddad wasn't mechanically blessed, and Fay was nearby and a generous helper son. He knew how to farm. But Grandpa was good to Fay, too. At the time of the uranium boom in southwestern Colorado and San Juan County, Utah, Fay ventured into the boom, as did many other successful farmers. He persuaded Grandpa to join in his uranium speculation. But uranium for most of those who put their money and property down and took the risk expecting great returns, there were few winners. For Fay and Grandpa, the uranium venture collapsed and Fay and Granddad, but especially Fay, took a great loss. Fay's family lived at the Gage farm for a while and Fay did most of the farming. Fay and his family were so good to Grandpa and appreciated how his needs increased, as he grew older.

Fay was a finishing carpenter and had to leave farming and work where finishing carpenters were needed. Often that was distant from Monticello and the family.

Wilmer and Lorena Dickens and their two sons moved to their farm home, just north of the Gage place, in the late forties. They were very religious and a Christian family with their behaviors was hard to find. Their farmland was a considerable distance from their modest home.

The Dickens discovered immediately that Grandpa was not an independent farmer. He lacked skills that enabled a modern farmer to be independent: welding, tractor and implement repairing, along with not owning the equipment to complete the growing and harvesting of crops that were planted. Grandpa became very dependent on Wilmer Dickens, and the other Dickens, too. The sons would regularly check on Grandpa. Wilmer was so helpful to Grandpa and others, that he overextended his commitment to help friends and neighbors' farm.

It was a year in the 1950s, deep into October and Grandpa was still relying on Wilmer to get to the threshing of his beans. Snow came, covered the stacked beans, and they rotted. Grandpa lost the entire crop. Wilmer was too committed to helping others. Grandpa said he didn't always take care of his own crops. For too much goodwill, Grandpa and others paid a price. Though our granddad lamented his loss to us, and probably to others, Wilmer was so liked and understood for his Christian goodwill, that Grandpa's lamentations were certainly not heard by the Dickens.

Our granddad died December 28, 1965, one day short of being eighty-five. A testimony of him being a farmer was that at eighty-four he was still farming his beans and hoed the entire bean crop, nearly two hundred acres, all by himself. It was the summer before his December death. He was living with his dear brother Basil in Tulsa. He died quickly following a massive heart attack. He was buried beside his wife, Effie, at the Dove Creek Cemetery.

John and Effie Gage. (Photograph from the trunk)

John and Effie Gage's grave marker at the Dove Creek Cemetery.
(Photograph by Joy Keown, July 2019)

7

HARDSHIPS OF GETTING AN EDUCATION
AND TEACHING IN ONE-ROOM RURAL SCHOOLS

In August of 1959 Bernice (Gage) Keown received her Bachelor of Arts Degree from Western State College in Gunnison, Colorado. She was fifty years old. Several in her family were there to witness and support her achievement that had been a journey of tenacity, determination, and overcoming a mountain of impediments. Her college career began at Fort Lewis Junior College in 1929. It was located at the historic Fort Lewis U.S. Army Fort near the little community of Hesperus, sixteen miles west of Durango, Colorado. She entered the school year 1929-30 with her sister Lura. The college was moved to Durango in 1956, the year my sister Beverly entered the college. It became a four-year institution in 1964.

In front of Taylor Hall at Western State College (now Western Colorado University), our mother is seen in graduation regalia with her diploma. Members of her family from left to right are: Grandpa John Gage, daughters Beverly and Barbara, and husband Herald. Her son, Duane (this author), took the photograph. (Beverly [Keown] Donovan photos)

Mother's Colorado education began the Monday after the family set foot in their Bug Point home on Halloween in 1923. They had passed by the school only days before. The Big Valley School was five miles from their very isolated home, the one without water.

Big Valley School has long been gone but it was at the intersection of County Roads 4 and N. (Photograph by Joy Keown, July 2019)

In 1923 Bryan was eighteen and his schooling had ended in Missouri. The old truck was put to use again for water and for transportation to school. It was a memorable time at Big Valley for the Gage kids and the names of friends made in 1923 came up often as mother recalled the days. We especially heard of the Livingston sisters, Lois, Doris and Jessie. Their mother, Mary Livingston, was a college graduate who later became the Dolores County Superintendent of Schools. But attendance at the Big Valley School was for only that single school year. Grandpa bought a homestead four and a half miles west of Dove Creek. At the end of the summer in 1924, five of the six children enrolled at the Dove Creek School.

Dove Creek School, the first school in Dove Creek, was built in 1921. It wasn't a one-room school, it had two rooms. Gage children enrolled in Dove Creek School at the end of summer in 1924. (Photograph from Montezuma's Trails of Time by Molly Warren)

Dan Hunter is a well-remembered pioneer in the Dove Creek country. He taught schools in the Dove Creek District for sixteen years and with R.T. Williams, gave Dove Creek its first newspaper in 1940, the *Dove Creek Press*. (Photograph from Montezuma's Trails of Time by Molly Warren)

The first Dove Creek School is remembered by the Gages and most of the other students of the school for its exceptional teacher, Dan Hunter. He was an enthusiastic teacher who promoted schools and education in the community and region. And he was an entrepreneur. With R.T, Williams he became the owner and first publisher of the weekly *Dove Creek Press* in 1940. Before then, he built the Hunter Hotel.

Dan was a World War I vet and with his wife, Loula, came to Dove Creek from Dallas, Texas in 1918. He claimed a homestead near Dove Creek and grubbed out the sage. He was tireless. The Colorado Historical Society called him "Sagebrush Dan." He founded the Dove Creek High School, organized the municipal water and power utilities, and when pinto beans came in as the natural profit crop for the cleared Great Sage Plains, he was a successful farmer.

As an author, he was known for his promotional articles in his *Dove Creek Press* about the western Dolores County country and his unique way of writing about the news and his opinions. He was a teacher for sixteen years in the Dove Creek District and influenced the futures of many students. Mother had many superlatives when she talked about Dan Hunter.

Before he founded the high school in Dove Creek, he added two years to the elementary school, grades nine and ten. Mother was able to enter the Cortez High School as an eleventh grader. When Mom became a teacher herself, she must have reflected on how Dan Hunter would teach his students and handle Dove Creek School. Below is a report by Dan Hunter in his *Dove Creek Press* about a stranded Galloping Goose on Lizard Head Pass on rails of the Rio Grande Southern Railroad. It gives the flavor of his writing. It is dated March 15, 1944. It describes a storm that snowbound Rico. A personal story about the storm is told later. We lived in Rico at the time.

Dan Hunter covers Galloping Goose. "The fiercest snowstorm of the century" swept across the Lizard Head Pass, marooning Mr. and Mrs. Fred Johnson and a three year-old grandson. The Johnsons live at Montrose, the grandson hails from Wyoming.

The bus, which is called the Galloping Goose, pulled out of Rico early Monday morning. The Goose was being towed by a Durango and Rio Grande Southern engine, which stalled about four miles west of Lizard Head snow sheds. The engineer, fireman and the Goose herder, realizing their dangerous and precarious condition used a portable telephone to hello Rico for food supplies and other relief. Men mounted snowshoes and slowly threaded their trailing up the snow-covered pass knowing that a crack of the whip might trigger an avalanche of snow and ice that might bury them beneath a thousand pounds of mountain debris. Nothing daunted these bold mountaineers, and about nine p.m. Monday, the weary, laden mountain climbers deposited food at the feet of the famishing Galloping Goose. My, what a spread and such a feast!

Wednesday morning, reports came that the rotary snowplow had not reached the marooned parties. Rollin Usher of Cortez and Milton Morgan nosed the Usher plane toward the stars in their dangerous mercy flight to bring further relief to those who were asunder upon a drift of snow and ice.

Ed Hunter and Joe Piccone, flying aces of Cortez, flew within the wake of the Usher plane as each phantom ship circled the snow-capped summit of old Lizard Head, dropping their heavenly parcel into the lap of the Galloping Goose.

When Mom entered the Cortez High School in 1927 it was about the same distance from Dove Creek as Dolores High School. The extra years, grades nine and ten in Dove Creek, enabled her to be an eleventh grader in Cortez. Her sister Lura, two years younger, entered high school the same year. Lura, Aunt Charlie as we called her, would be a ninth grader and enrolled in the Dolores High School.

Mother took Latin two years at Cortez High School. She always said she had four years of Latin. Were there two years of Latin at Dove Creek? Why would she, how could she, take four years of Latin at the Cortez High School? She acknowledged it was her love for her teacher, Anna Henry. Anna Henry was a long time teacher at Cortez High School and remembered by Mom as her favorite teacher. It wasn't just Mom who studied the dead language for two years, there were many, because of Anna Henry.

I am sure Mrs. Henry was aware that mother was a dry lander and she knew of her privations and that she had to leave home to get a high school education. She and her sister had few clothes, and in my own experience, for five years a high school teacher led me to know of the petty society and cliques that exist among teenagers. There are traits of that age, and were extant in the 1920s, too. I knew Anna Henry late in her life, long after her retirement, as she was the older aunt of my best high school friend, Jim Henry. Her loving ways and impartial acceptance of each person just carried on.

Mom lived with two Cortez families while attending Cortez High School those two years. I only remember the name of one family, but both became her dear friends. Years later when our family moved from Rico to Cortez, one in particular, Mrs. Owens, would come to see us. Her husband had passed away, but she continued to live on the farm close to Cortez where Mom boarded and helped the family with farm chores. Her friendship and individuality need a few sentences.

Anna Henry (Photograph from *Cortez* by Vila Schwindt, Janet Weeth, and Dale Davidson)

Mary (Hendrickson) Owens was born in Goose Creek, Iowa in 1878 and came to Montezuma County from Delta, Colorado, by way of Telluride and Rico in 1909. With her husband, Louis Owens, they purchased and developed the farm where Mom boarded, just north of Cortez. She had been a teacher in Iowa. To say she was eccentric would not be an exaggeration. When she would come to visit us in the late 1940s and 50s, Mom said she had not changed a bit. She was old when we met her, and certainly not a slave to fashion. She wore old clothes that were of another generation, a stocking cap, and always seemed so glad to see her former teenage boarder. And though she was very opinionated, hers and mother's friendship endured until she died.

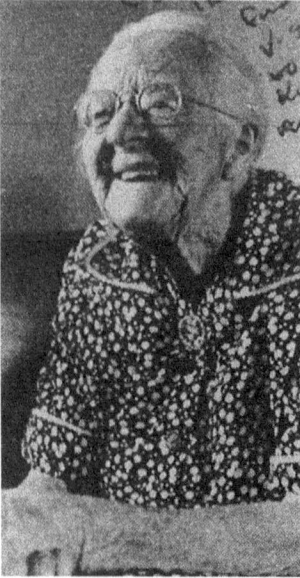

Mary Lettie (Hendrickson) Owens. (Photograph from the *Cortex Sentinel*)

In 1929 mother graduated from Cortez High School. For reasons that were never explained to us, or maybe we never asked, Aunt Lura attended Dolores High School, twelve miles to the north of Cortez. But at the end of summer in 1929 they both entered Fort Lewis College. Most colleges then, and continue today, admit students who can handle the classes. My daughter, Julie, entered the University of Wyoming without graduating from high school. A short time later, she was a professor at the University of Wisconsin.

Where money came from for the Gage sisters to attend college, for even the one year, I don't know. It was two years before Grandpa became the Dolores County Sheriff and certainly he was poor that year, not even money for a car. Mother told us she and Aunt Charlie and Lois and Doris Livingston, schoolmates from Big Valley and Dove Creek, rented a little house near the campus. To help pay rent, they wallpapered the place for the owner.

It was only a year at Fort Lewis for Mom and Aunt Charlie. At twenty Mother became the teacher of the Peel School, about ten miles northwest of Dove Creek. And Aunt Charlie would have only been seventeen and later on, in 1932, she became one of two teachers at the High Hill School, five miles southwest of Dove Creek.

Teachers of the Colorado and other Rocky Mountain state rural schools in those days were to meet the expectations of local school boards and parents. From a series about Morgan County Colorado one-room schools, "Portraits of the Past: Revisiting the days of one-room schools," the expectations are articulated. Certainly, they were those for Dolores County also. "Typically, 60% to 80% of the rural schoolteachers were young, unmarried women and expected to serve their community as the personification of Wisdom and Virtue." Bernice Gage and Aunt Lura met and lived up to those standards.

Much of Mother's life following the year at Fort Lewis is taken from an essay Dad wrote and used when he spoke in 1975 at mother's retirement party. It was after Mother had taught for 20 years in the Cortez School District.

In 1930, Peel School was Mother's first one-room, multi grade teaching position. The Fort Lewis classes were not preparation for teaching, but the general studies classes most students take the freshman year. But in those days, a single year of college was considered adequate to teach elementary school. College educations were almost nonexistent among parents of early Dove Creek country. Even in the 1920s and 30s, parents were expected to send their children to school. But were teachers expected to have fifty-four students in a one-room school and teach eight grades? This was the situation by spring in 1931 for Mother. The Great Depression had set in and a steady influx of Dust Bowlers and other depression refugees just kept coming. She had begun the school year with about twenty pupils.

Probably outdoor recess was canceled on this snowy winter day at the Peel School about 1931. The trip to the outhouse must have been an adventure. (Photograph from *Montezuma Trails of Time* by Molly Warren)

By spring, students ranged in age from six to sixteen. The best testimony about the effect of the depression was Mom's description of some students that would walk as far or farther than she did to school. For some, over-boots for the snow-covered path would have been way beyond the family means. They walked to school with their worn shoes wrapped in gunnysacks and binder twine was wound around the sacks to hold the sack in place. When they arrived, the sacks came off and were allowed to dry during the school day. Their feet were bound again for the walk home. Even a more revealing testament to the times was what some children carried to lunch in a paper bag that went home each day and was used for several days. It was a single ear of corn that had been dried but made edible by soaking.

When the students left for home, our mom became the janitor. The mud carried in from the students' walk to the school and two recesses required both a broom and a shovel. The shovel was used to scoop the pile of dried mud swept to the front door. She began the walk to her room at the school board president's home. Mom said she was sure the school board president was illiterate.

Dinner was with the school board president's family. Her sleeping room at the home was an addition to the home that was cobbled up and tacked to the house. There were cracks in the walls and cold air would blow in. Breakfast was early with the family and then it was the long walk to the school. I am sure she wondered about what the size of the student population would be that day. Mary Livingston, who was the Dolores County School Superintendent during Mom's Peel School experience, later told Dad, "Nobody but a bull-headed girl like Bernice would have stuck it out the way she did. They would have walked away."

For a year after teaching at Peel School, Mom worked with the family on the farm. In 1932 she became the teacher at Coal Bed School near the rural community of Northdale, about five miles southwest of Dove Creek. Conditions for teaching at Coal Bed were vastly better than those she endured at the Peel School. It was school teaching in the 1930s and the paddle was then appropriate for a higher level of misbehavior. Mom used it once. I will attest that in the forties it was still in use by my fourth grade teacher. I was paddled twice. Dad related this story of Mom's use of the paddle at the Coal Bed School when he spoke at her retirement party.

Bernice Gage Keown at age twenty-one. The photograph was taken the year she taught at the Peel School. (From Beverly Keown personal photos)

The building had a tin roof and one day during lunch hour some boys, including one age seventeen, were throwing rocks on the roof and watching them slide off. She warned the boys. Students had no more entered the school at the end of lunchtime and another big rock landed on the roof. Mother asked the class, "Who threw that rock?" The students looked at the seventeen year-old eighth grader. Years later, this same boy and another former student, now young men, visited the Keown home in Rico. As they were leaving, the one who had thrown the rock, laughingly made the remark, "All right George, you disobeyed me and now you can take the consequences," which were the very words mother had said before she used the paddle.

George is probably the tallest boy in the back row at the Coal Bed School in 1933. He was seventeen and the final rock thrower. Mom enjoyed teaching at the school. She is the woman (Miss Gage then) at the right, second row. (Photograph from *Montezuma's Trails of Time* by Molly Warren)

Here I will add that from 1932–1933 Aunt Charlie was a teacher at High Hill School, southwest of Dove Creek. She was eighteen when Mom began teaching at Peel.

The Fairview School at Yellow Jacket, Colorado was Mom's last one-room school. Fairview School was in Montezuma County and must have been the school of the least of her one-room school memorable school events. She talked about the many fine students and their supportive parents. A most memorable event that school year occurred on December 1, 1934 when she married my dad. Dad was going on his fourth year as County Treasurer of Dolores County and lived in Rico.

In 1933, ten years after the Gages landed at Bug Point in 1923, this photograph of the High Hill School was taken. The woman second from left is Aunt Lura who became a teacher at the High Hill School. She was twenty-two in 1933. She and my mother both taught one-room schools with one year of college preparation at Fort Lewis College near Durango. Note the structure of the school. It tells of the time and the economy. Instead of sawed lumber, vertical logs were used. In 1933, the country was deep into the Great Depression. (Photograph from *Montezuma's Trails of Time* by Molly Warren)

After a festive wedding shivaree at the school, staged by parents, Mom finished the school year and in the Spring went to the home Dad prepared for in Rico. There were a total of three wedding shivarees: Fair View School, Dove Creek and Rico.

Mom gave birth to her three children in three years, 1936, 1937, and 1938. It need not be explained that she valued education. Rico did not have a high school. Teaching school would not continue again for nearly twenty years, until all of us kids were in high school in Cortez. It was her anticipation that we three might be in college at the same time, and Dad's salary would not keep us in college. For me, after their help for the freshman and sophomore years, I left college and followed an oil seismograph crew to Alaska for over a year and saved money.

Employment opportunities and pay for women today has changed some, but sadly, not enough. In the fifties employment and pay for men and women wasn't even comparable. Barbara and Beverly needed more help than I did for college.

With anticipation of the college situation for her children, Mother began substitute teaching for elementary school grades in the Cortez School District. She also took extension and correspondence classes, one after the other. When I was a high school junior in 1954 she went back to Fort Lewis College for a second year of preparation to teach. Fort Lewis College was still a junior college in 1954. We were all supporters in her return to college, especially Dad. We all pitched in. Becoming a teacher with a full time position was Mom's twenty-four hours a day, seven-day-a-week obsession—except for Sundays, eleven a.m. to twelve p.m. when she attended the service at the Baptist Church. She was in high gear and no impediments would get in her way.

Cortez was thirty-four miles from Fort Lewis College. Mom was home each weekend. She prepared food to go into the refrigerator for our meals; carried out her class assignments, and early Monday morning was ready for her ride to the Fort. The ride was with Cortez students who came home for the weekends. As I recall, they were all boys, young, and they seemed uninterrupted by their forty-five year-old passenger. Of course, she paid at least her fare for the ride. Some had been older members of athletic teams I played on at Cortez High School.

During the week at Fort Lewis, mother lived with Miss Hershberger, a single English professor. I remember well the textbook Mom used for her Zoology class. It was especially thick for a 1954 text (They have grown thicker and more expensive over time). I used it to supplement my preparation for high school and college biology teaching. At the end of each chapter were interesting facts about the group (Orders) of organisms the chapter had covered: such as the largest whale on record, possible ancestors of birds, just bits of interesting information that grabbed students' interest.

After the school year at Fort Lewis, Mom was still a long way from a degree and although other qualified teacher candidates were available, in 1955 she was offered, and accepted, a full-time position teaching second graders at Downey Elementary School. It had been her reputation as a substitute teacher that gave Mom a lead on other candidates. After two years at Downey, mother asked to be transferred to Manaugh School, which was only a block from our home at 231 South Washington. The transfer was approved and for eighteen more years she taught second grade at Manaugh. During those years she came home with stories from her classroom.

There was the time when a little student in her class was absent for a time with hepatitis. A student in her class asked her if the student with hepatitis was coming back. Mother said, "It might be a while, he has hepatitis."

"What's that?" another child asked.

"It's a disease of the liver," Mom told the class.

A little boy spoke out, "I'll never get hepatitis," he said. "I never eat liver. I hate it."

Many more extension classes, correspondence classes, and summer sessions were completed until the summer session at Western State College was over in 1959 and she received her Bachelor of Arts degree.

I recently found a paper online that she wrote in 1964, after her graduation, as an assignment for a summer workshop at Adams State College in Alamosa. The workshop was titled, Colorado Indian Education and the director was Mamie Sizemore. Each student of the workshop submitted a paper. Mom's was titled, "The Ute Mountain Utes." When bussing of students on Indian Reservations to boarding schools ended, Ute Mountain Tribe children began attending Cortez schools. Even after she received her degree, as a true professional, her preparation to teach continued.

If three words describe Mom they are dedication, tenacity and work: dedication to her children, her husband, and education; tenacity—she just wouldn't quit; and work, from the day's beginning until her time to go to bed, which was late. She seemed to never take a break. Sunday afternoons she would grab the Denver Post, and read the news and the funnies. In my life, especially as an adult, when I hit low points, as we all do, and needed inspiration, I looked no further than to my mother.

8

COURTSHIP, MARRIAGE, AND LIFE IN RICO

Courtship leading to marriage for Herald Keown and Bernice Gage in 1934 may be the shortest topic addressed in this book. In 1932, Dad was the most eligible bachelor in Dolores County.

He was single, the County Treasurer, and thirty-five years old. He had never been married but his age may have caused questions for twenty-year-old women, and especially parents of twenty-year-olds. But just as important as other qualifications, with elections he had a continuing job and it was the Great Depression. Bernice Gage was pretty, had a year of college, a job if she wanted it again, and was twenty years old.

Where or when Mom and Dad met in 1930 we do not know, but it was in 1930 and she was the teacher at Peel School. Dad had just been elected Dolores County Treasurer. We can only speculate. Though Dad was full of stories, his courtship with Mom was not one of them. The very brief story I tell comes from my sister, Beverly, and it was from Mom to her.

Community members of mixed ages—all ages—often met at dances. They were social events important to folks who lived far apart, and we are the compulsive communicators. Both of our parents talked of the dances with great memories. The ones Mom attended were in the Dove Creek region. Though Dad lived in Rico where the courthouse was, he was caring for his elderly parents on the homestead and returned there often, considering the roads and times. Our parents both liked to dance. We assume they met at a dance. Also encouraging the friendship was John Gage, who was sheriff of Dolores County beginning in 1931, the same year Dad assumed his elected position.

Mom accepted an engagement ring from Dad when she was twenty. But neither Mom nor Dad ever told us why she gave it back. Of course, we do speculate. There were twelve years difference in age. Though Mom had endured tough times and was more mature than most girls of twenty, she was still only twenty. Dad had been his own boss and was head of his affairs and his elderly parents' affairs for a while. I think it was the age difference and probably his desire to "run the show" that caused the ring to be returned. Dad and I had conversations, but they were never about his past love life. It was sports news, political happenings, and Cortez events, but never about his past love life, nor mine. He was very brief in advice for me; even too brief. But once he told me, "Don't wait as long as I did to get married."

There was harmony after the breakup and the Gages still invited Dad to family gatherings. That is the short of our parents' courtship story, except to say that on December 1, 1934 they eloped and were married in Pagosa Springs, Colorado. Mother told my sister Beverly one rather unimportant detail about the Pagosa Springs wedding. "It was raining in Pagosa Springs and the rain caused my hair to curl for my wedding picture." That was all she said.

But there were details that went into local newspapers about Mom and Dad's wedding. There were three parties that followed. The first was at Yellow Jacket, the community of the Fairview School where she was teaching at the time. The parents sponsored it. Another was at Dove Creek where they were both well-known, and third, in Rico, Dad's home where she would join him.

It seemed that though it was an elopement, there were expectations they would one day be married and there would be celebrations to go with their union.

Wedding picture of Mother and Dad. Had Mom not told my sister that her hair curled in the Pagosa Springs rain that afternoon of December 1, 1934, we would not have known it, nor would we have cared. It is just like our memories of them. (Photograph from the trunk)

In Rico the newlyweds first lived in a rented house near the courthouse. But soon Dad traded his DeSoto car for a house in West Rico. West Rico consisted of a group of eight homes across the Dolores River, about a quarter of a mile from the Rio Grande Southern Rico Depot. We have always called it the Little Yellow House.

From the house Dad always walked to the courthouse, about half a mile away. Below is the house as it looked in the summer of 2019. Dad sold it in 1944 for $1,500 to a Texas couple. Since our family left Rico, owners of the "Little Yellow House" have continued improvements and it has been a summer home.

The "Little Yellow House" in Rico hasn't been yellow for years but time has been good to it. West Rico has flushing toilets, unlike our time there when all eight of the houses of the addition had outhouses. Though I lived there less than seven years, it holds many memories. I was born in a home across the street. Dad traded his DeSoto car for the house in 1935. (Photograph by Joy Keown, July 2019)

What about the town of Rico where Herald Keown took his new bride? It was depression time in 1934 and the population of Rico was at low ebb. The life of the town was always a roller coaster, ever since the Enterprise Lode was struck in 1887 by David Swickhimer. He continues to be the most celebrated miner ever in the mining town. He and his miners were digging a shaft just southeast of the mining camp with literally his last money, and his hired help were working for a share of minerals that might be discovered.

Swickhimer hit it big in his Enterprise Mine. Ultimately he became rich, Rico's first millionaire. He built a bank, and the Enterprise Hotel on the main street, and remains Rico's most philanthropic quick-rich-and-then-busted citizen. Rico was at its zenith in 1892 and in the area there were 5,000 people. The records say there were twenty-three saloons, two newspapers, two churches, a theatre, boarding houses, and three blocks of red light districts. Hotel Enterprise and the Rico Bank burned in 1903. Rico lived in cycles based upon the price and the national need for minerals.

In 1935 Mother met Rico at the height, or should we say the low point, of the Great Depression. And it would not come alive again until the U.S. began to prepare for World War II. May 5, 1936 Barbara, my older sister, was born in Cortez at the Johnson Hospital. The hospital was named for a Cortez doctor who served the entire Montezuma and Dolores Counties, even to make house calls to the Keown homestead at Dove Creek. I was born at a home across the street from the Little Yellow House and the doctor was the Rico Argentine Mining Company's company doctor. His name was Dr. Coplowitz, who a few years later became a well-known ophthalmologist located in Durango. But on the night of June 22, 1937 he reported to the house across from the Yellow House where I was about to be born.

Joe Lewis, the Brown Bomber, was set to fight Jim Braddock for the World Heavyweight Championship. Dr. Coplowitz and Dad were both fight fans and it was at night when good radio reception was waited for in the valley town. Coplowitz and Dad were glued to the radio and Mom was in labor in the bedroom. Dad and the doctor had split their attention. Lewis knocked out Braddock in the eighth round, just about the round of labor when I was born. Joe Lewis went on to defend his crown twenty-five times and held the crown the longest in any weight division, from that June 22 night until March 1, 1947. With Dad, and I don't know about Coplowitz, we have an event that corresponds with my birth. Mom didn't like having to share the attention that night. In that little town the word soon got out about the dissimilar, but parallel, events.

My older sister, Barbara, was less than fourteen months old when I was born. Sixteen months after I was born, my younger sister, Beverly, was born. It was October 26, 1938. Mother was pregnant and caring for kids nearly all of the years we were in Rico. She did not learn to enjoy Rico or attach to that small county-seat community as Dad had grown to love.

First let's look at Rico by the frame of reference in which Dad saw the town. He was a Rico baseball team member and an exceptional player. He was elected by a large majority of votes to be the County Treasurer. In wartime he held the position as head of Rico's security. He traded with merchants and daily walked to work through the town to the courthouse. His position as treasurer gave him exchange each day with the Rico residents, as well as folks from around the county.

Though Rico had its booms and busts, there was a core population that were together to serve and make the town an enjoyable site for most to live. They worked as a community together. I will focus on one family, the Alfred (Alf) Baer family. The Baers were miners and as young men, the brothers all lived in Rico. The road to Dunton, a ghost mining town at the head of the West Dolores River, goes over the Meadows Pass. The road that leaves the East Dolores canyon to the Meadows is one lane with many switchbacks and is dangerous, even today. Alf Baer and his brother Charlie were coming down into East Dolores in 1932 when their vehicle went off a switchback curve and rolled almost to the road, near the river. Charlie was crushed and died. Alf crawled to the road where he was seen and taken to Rico and then to the Cortez Hospital. His injuries were critical: broken vertebra, and ribs torn from his spine. Dr. Johnson cared for him, along with a nurse, Allie Meadows. Alf spent a long time in the hospital, long enough to be smitten by Allie. Alf recovered, married Allie, and took her to Rico in 1933. My dad took his bride to Rico in 1935.

Allie (Meadows) Baer at twenty-five. Alf probably knew what a treasure he had brought to Rico, but soon after, the community also realized what a gem he was sharing with the isolated mining town. (Photograph from Glen Baer)

Allie began service to the poor and the sick prior to Mother Teresa becoming recognized by the world. Allie Baer's tireless service to the ill, injured, and pregnant, along with her consoling comfort to mourners of those who died, was known up and down the Dolores River Valley. Some spoke of her as the Mother Teresa of Rico. Without a doubt, for most of her life she was the most admired and respected person in Rico. From her humble home she met and nursed the medical needs of people from all cultures, often without payment. Her son, and my lifelong friend, Glen Baer, tells me the story of a particular example of her tireless dedication and courage.

Late on a snowy evening, about midnight, a young Hispanic man knocked on the front door of the Baer's house. He kept knocking. Allie slept in a bedroom near the back of the home, a long way from the front door, and didn't hear the knocking. Glen and his brother slept in a second story bedroom just above the front door.

The fellow kept knocking and Glen put his head out the window and asked the guy what he wanted. He told Glen his wife was having a hard time delivering a baby and she really needed help. Glen woke his mother. She put on snow pants and boots, and with the young man began wading through the snow that was about a foot deep. The home of the desperate man was in West Rico near the railroad depot, nearly half a mile from the Baer home. Hispanic people of Rico lived together across the railroad tracks from the depot, several in old converted boxcars. Boxcars made very compromised one-room living spaces. Such was the home of the young man and his wife.

The young wife was very stressed, and Allie took over. She worked with the delivery way into the morning. While tending with the difficult delivery, the young husband began fixing a breakfast in the kitchen end of the boxcar. The delivery was finally successful, the young wife was recovering, and breakfast was ready. Allie had breakfast with the young father, and he said he didn't have money to pay her. But he did have a six-pack of beer that he wanted her to take. She told him, "I don't drink but my husband does." She took the beer.

Allie met all kinds of medical circumstances in those forty plus years, and she was Rico's first line of medical service. There were mining accidents, broken bones, and influenza. For her patients with severe pain she administered morphine, and she gave shots for childhood diseases. She readied severe cases, those that needed hospitalization, for the trip to the Cortez Hospital or the Telluride Hospital. For those hospital cases it had to be a Rico a resident that provided the transportation. The town of Rico didn't have a city ambulance until the fifties.

One emergency that her son, Glen, tells me about called for resourcefulness and Allie's attention for days. It was August 19, 1944. Edgar and Mavis Branson called Allie when Mavis was about to deliver a child. Mavis knew it was way too soon. Allie knew the newborn would be very premature, so she prepared.

There wasn't an incubator in all of Rico, and certainly the distance from the isolated town to a hospital was too great, and the time of travel would be too long for a very immature infant to survive. Mavis delivered the baby and the little girl was estimated to weigh about two pounds. Allie put the baby into a shoebox lined with cloth. Then she put the shoebox into a regular stove oven at its lowest temperature and with constant attention the oven was kept at 98 degrees, the same temperature as the mother's womb. What was the source of fuel for the ordinary kitchen stove? Most Rico residents in those days used wood or coal. The little girl named Phyllis survived and was healthy. Sadly though, she died early at only twenty in Durango, on March 20, 1964.

Let me relate another early birth in a very small mining town, smaller than Rico, Ophir. I was at a booth in the Ute Café in Cortez with two friends of mine, Adrian Fisher and Dick O'Connel, with whom I worked with in the Dolores District of San Juan National Forest. It was in the summer of 1961. The waitress was a woman about sixty. She must not have been really busy because she sat down in the booth with us and when she learned we worked in the Rico area she said she was born in Ophir. Who is born in Ophir? The tiny mining settlement is at 10,000 feet.

"I was born premature," she said. Then she told about her parents and the midwife putting her in a canning boiler container and they kept warm bricks all around it. She grew up healthy. She looked very healthy and certainly friendly, doing the work of a waitress in a normally busy cafe.

During active mining days Rico had company doctors paid by large mining companies. They served all patients, miners, or not. The doctors at my birth and my younger sister Beverly's birth were company doctors.

The little white house at the left of the Community Church was the home and office of company doctor George Sprecher, the doctor who attended the birth of my younger sister, Beverly. (Photograph from *The Rio Grande Southern Story*, Volume 5, "Rico and the Mines")

But when the mining economy of Rico was in a slump, doctors of Telluride, and one later from Cortez, made weekly trips to Rico. Allie took care of Rico people with these doctors' supervision. A medical doctor from Telluride was the very respected Dr. Parker. Later, the Cortez doctor was Dr. Merritt, who was paid by miners at the Rico Argentine Mining company. A ten dollar monthly fee, deducted from the miners' pay, paid for care of ailments and visits with Merritt. To serve as Merritt's Rico nurse, the very wealthy doctor paid Allie a pittance.

Mother Teresa of Rico and her husband, Alf, had three children. The oldest is her daughter Elaine, and then sons Glen, and Max. Today they all live in Cortez. Alfred (Alf) worked in mines or mills all of his life. He died of miner con (silicosis), on March 11, 1968, and Allie lived another eighteen years and died August 26, 1986.

Glen Baer and his late wife Louise. They have two sons, Jeff and Alfred. Louise died February 29, 2016. Glen has been a lifelong friend and an important contributor to these Rico accounts. He and I attended the first grade in Rico and were classmates at the Montezuma-Cortez High School. Glen remarried.
(Photograph from Glen)

Let me tell a story from Glen about a classmate, Bill Ince, in Rico when the two were in the third grade. Later the same year in Cortez, Bill was a classmate of mine. Bill had a propensity for trouble and those who chummed with him became associates in trouble and suffered the same, or worse, consequences.

Glen had a new bb gun. Glen and Bill were looking for targets in Rico when they came to a home and property where the owner kept goats. Bill took Glen's bb gun and shot a goat, only stinging it. The act was seen by the owner of the goats and he hurried to the source of the shot. He grabbed the bb gun and broke it into two pieces over his knee and handed it back. Did Glen tell his folks what happened to the gun? I don't know. Bill's family moved to Cortez while Bill was in the third grade and I first became acquainted with him.

In our junior high years in Cortez, Bill led me to misdeeds that I would not have done on my own. We were not caught and if we had been, the consequences would have been worse than a bb gun broken into pieces. I will not leave Bill here as a bad apple. He was a friend. I cannot deny my lack of foresight in stunts when he was the leader. He was an undisciplined only child and the best all-around athlete in our high school of more than 500 students.

When our classmate, Frank Humpreys, sustained a knee injury as a sophomore in high school football, Bill became the fastest runner in the school. In 1954, Durango tied with Lamar for the Colorado football championship, seven to seven. When we were playing our rival Durango that year, they were beating us badly. Bill took the ball at midfield, got into the Durango backfield and outran them all in a dash to score our only touchdown.

The memories of my life in Rico are fuzzy since I was young and lived there only seven years, June of 1937 to June of 1944. I'll go back in time. My sister Barbara attended the first and second grade and I was in the first grade at the old brick school that was built in 1892.

A vivid memory was an afternoon recess in the winter and with other kids of all ages, grades one through eight, we were sliding down a slope east of the school with improvised sleds of all kinds. It was my turn to slide down the slope in a large dishpan. The pan was whirling around as it went down the slope and I was thrown out, landing on my forehead. My forehead began to swell, and I guess my behavior was suspect because Mrs. Tuller, my teacher, took me to Dad's office at the courthouse about two blocks from the school. I walked home with Dad, and for Mom, Dad and myself (and at the time), it was the end of the story.

When I was in the fourth grade and not doing well in reading, my folks took me to Dr. Calkins, a Cortez physician who also did eye testing. He alarmed my parents. He suspected I had eye damage from the collision with the ground (or was it packed snow?). I wore glasses soon after the eye test and on a test given to fourth graders at the beginning of the grade and at the end of the grade, I made the most progress of Lucile Henry's students. Lucile Henry was the sister of Anna Henry, Mom's favorite teacher of them all. Lucile Henry was the teacher who gave me two paddlings. Could that have helped me see better?

The story about our little chickens is hard to believe, but for this one I am a witness. Probably because of Mom's farmer background that she didn't let go easy, we had new baby chicks in our West Rico backyard—and ducks—but that is another story.

When Dad walked in from work one late Spring afternoon, he was carrying one of the baby chickens. He said he picked up the chicken about a hundred yards from the house on his walk home, but he said there were more and that he would go after them. Mom told him there had been a whirlwind that she heard from within the house. It scattered debris against the north side of the house. It just rattled the side of the house, she said. Dad went back and picked up some more chicks. We've all heard the expression, "It's raining cats and dogs," but up the road north of the Keown house for a very brief moment that day it rained (or the whirlwind dropped) some baby chicks.

Let's get to the duck story. I don't think our folks bought the ducks for Easter; rather, for the family to eat once they grew up. They did grow up and were even given names. We had a woven wire fence around the place, and I remember how they would walk around the house in line, largest to smallest. Dad couldn't kill them, so he gave them to the Richards who lived over the Dolores River Bridge, near the rails of the Rio Grande Southern. Theirs was one of only a few wooden frame homes in the Hispanic addition of the town.

The Richards were older and poor. They invited our family to dinner. Perhaps Dad had made a previous arrangement with the Richards and they knew he had a hard time killing domestic animals, though he liked to hunt rabbits. But the dinner meal that evening was duck.

Rico is in a snow belt. The snow often gets three to five feet deep. It is 9,000 feet in elevation.

This photograph was taken in 1932 in Rico following a snow storm. It is the main street of Rico, Glasgow Avenue. Glen Baer's father, Alfred Baer, operated the pump most days, but maybe not this day. (Photograph from *The Rio Grande Southern Story*, Volume 5, "Rico and the Mines")

At the summit of Lizard Head Pass between Rico and Telluride there is a wide plain where the wind can push snow into deep drifts that even with plows, engines pulling trains were stopped. After the rail line was built from Rico to Telluride, the final solution to the Lizard Head Pass impediment was to build a long snow shed, about two hundred yards long where drifts were deepest. Trains would escape the drifts by going through the shed and the winds were strong enough to put drifts on top of the shed.

The same snowstorm that stranded a Galloping Goose rail truck with passengers in its bus compartment, had also snowbound Rico. It was in March of 1944. Several days of being snowbound began to worry Ricoites, and shelves at the two grocery stores were becoming bare. Word came that from the south a rotary snowplow was on its way to clear the track and let a train through with supplies for Rico. I remember well the crowd of Rico people, including our family, at the Rico Depot. We saw the sight of the rotary snowplow throwing snow into air as it came from the south into Rico. People clapped and yelled.

This is not the rotary snowplow that was celebrated that March afternoon in 1944. It is similar and it worked the Rio Grande Southern Railroad during the same time. (Photograph from *The Rio Grand Southern Story*, Volume 5)

I was only four and a half years old that Sunday and the event in 1941 is foggy in my mind, but it was that "Day of Infamy," December 7, 1941. Dad was putting a pole rail on the fence that surrounded the Little Yellow House. For December, it was an exceptionally balmy day and I was with him in the front yard. A car pulled up in front of our home. A fellow got out of his car and came into our front yard and talked to Dad.

The Japanese had bombed Pearl Harbor in Hawaii at about 11:55 a.m.

our time. At 7:55 a.m. Hawaii time, the bombing began. Dad was not his usual composed self and I followed him into the house where he told Mom. We were anxious for evening darkness when radio reception was good in that mountain valley town and we would get the bombing story. Our family was gathered around the table radio, a good one for that age. Of course, at four and a half, I didn't know the significance of why Mom and Dad seemed excited, and even stressed. Their unusual behavior is what I remember, and little did I know then what it meant to the world. Dad was Rico's Civil Defense Chairman.

It was a Zenith table model radio like this one that we used the night of December 7, 1941 to listen to news about the attack by Japan on Pearl Harbor. The radio was in use with the family for years, well into the 1950s. (Photograph from Zenith Table Model free photos)

The U.S, declared war on Japan December 8, 1941 and December 11, 1941 against Germany. Blackouts were scheduled events in towns of strategic importance. They actually began in 1939 when it became obvious the U.S. would have to join World War II. Regulations were imposed on September 1, 1939, before the declarations of war. These required that all windows and doors be covered at night with suitable material such as heavy curtains and cardboard to prevent the escape of any glimmer of light that might aid enemy aircraft.

Rico was a town where strategic metals were mined and on a national basis these were sites where blackouts were required. As the Director of Civil Defense for Rico, Dad scheduled a blackout and thoroughly spread the word of the night and time for the Rico blackout and the rules that went with blackouts. The canyon town that it was, mining roads came out and up the canyon sides. A main one was to the mill up Silver Creek. It rose in elevation quickly and the entire town of Rico could be viewed from above.

The designated time arrived, and the town went black. Up the Silver Creek mill road Dad went in his 1941 Chevy to where he could survey the town for blackout behavior. It was perfect—almost. In West Rico one house's lights were blazing. When he crossed the Dolores River Bridge it was easy to spot it. It was his own. Mom must have had a higher priority than a possible air raid. Whether Dad announced the "near perfect" success of the blackout to the town's people I don't know, but I can guess he didn't.

As I near the end of stories about our family's life in Rico, one event was with alarm. It called on the great compassion of the community, and especially the next-door neighbors in West Rico. They were tested in 1941.

Perhaps some mothers can hold up to having three babies in three years, but our mother was not one of them. She developed a fallen uterus. The medical condition is termed Uterine Prolapse. Muscles and ligaments around the uterus can weaken. When this support structure starts to fail, the uterus can sag out of position. In some cases, the uterus can slip out of position and into the birth canal, the vagina.

Where her condition was diagnosed, in Rico by the company doctor; a doctor in Cortez or Telluride doesn't matter. She needed surgery, a hysterectomy. The doctors of Cortez didn't want to do the surgery, for in those times it was surgery for a well-equipped hospital and a surgeon who knew well the hysterectomy process.

Durango, fifty miles east of Cortez and the Mercy Hospital was the location where Cortez doctors took their qualifying patients. So, Durango it was, and the surgery went well. Mom was in the hospital for three weeks. Today, as with most surgeries, hospitalization would not be twenty-one days. But her surgeon in 1941 must have been aware of where her home was: fifty miles north of Cortez on a mostly dirt road after traveling the fifty miles from Durango to Cortez. Being so far from emergency care, should there be complications, was just too dangerous.

We children stayed nights with Dad at the Little Yellow House, but before he headed up Depot Hill to go to the courthouse, he left us with West Rico neighbors. I was left at Edna and Erwin Dot's home. Their house in West Rico was two houses west of ours. They were examples of the caring community that surrounded us. I was four, Beverly was three, and Barbara was five. They were left each morning with Lorna and Jim Linton. They had a little girl, Lorna Lee, Beverly's age. Such friends who cared for us like children of their own were exemplary of the town where we lived. None of us were in school then to complicate Mom's absence. We were young and hardly remember the time with our daytime caretakers, and that is a compliment. In Mom's absence, one complaint I have heard about was from Beverly. At only three, she did not like the way Dad combed her hair.

Wonderful as our neighbors were, after the three weeks Mom was in the hospital, we rejoiced to have her back. And for Dad, who made a weekend trip to Durango while she was there, her homecoming and recovery was such a blessing. When we went to get her, I saw my first airplane up close at the Durango Airport. It was where Fort Lewis College is today. The photos below tell of family times in West Rico.

Dad holds the first born, Barbara, at our West Rico home the summer of 1937. (Photograph from the trunk)

Mom is holding Beverly in this photograph of us kids. That is our 1937 Chevy in the background. (Photograph from the trunk)

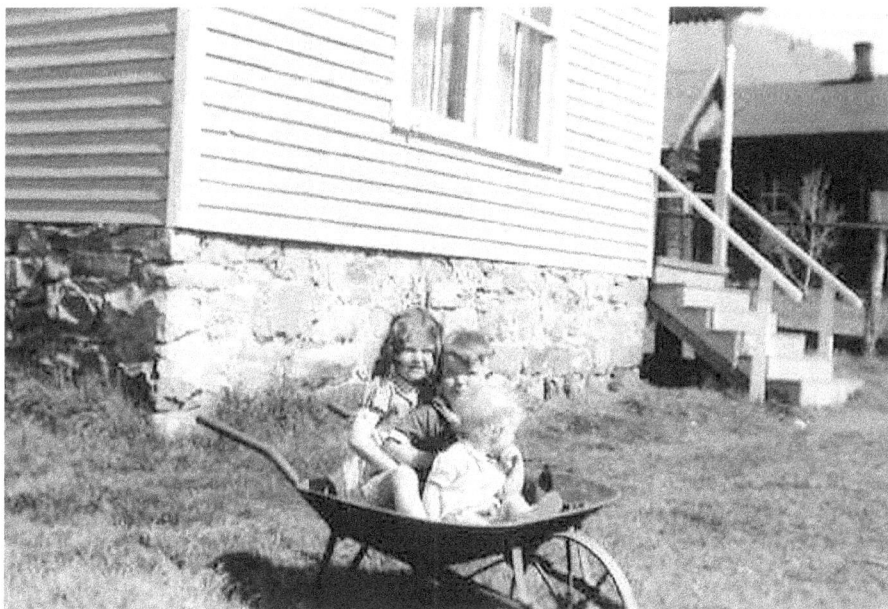

The three of us are ready for a ride in the wheelbarrow in this 1940 picture. The Little Yellow House is free of snow in this summer setting. (Photograph from the trunk)

Looking back in these pages, Dad's younger brother, Urban, hasn't occupied much space. He was the pitcher on Dove Creek's first baseball team. I remember him when he came to Rico and was employed as the tram operator for a mine on Silver Creek Road.

One evening while Urban was on shift we drove up to see just where he worked. The tram was right beside the road and ore in tramcars was dumped into trucks that emptied into railroad cars from a platform near the railroad depot. Urban's job was receiving the tramcars with ore and dumping the ore into dump trucks. Low and behold, in July of 2019 the relic of the tram operators station remains, and the rusted cable still reaches to the mine way up on the south side of Silver Creek.

Urban was in this tram house. It was way back in the early 1940s. Our family rode up Silver Creek Road to see him at his workstation. (Photograph by Joy Keown, July, 2019)

Urban had a history of successive jobs and didn't stay long with any. He even served one term as the Dolores County Assessor. With his wife, June, he had two children, my cousins Tom and Sandra (Sandy). Suzie was June's child when they were married and was adopted by Urban. Suzie was in California when my sister last saw her. Tom died relatively young, and Sandy became a successful music student and teacher who went to Fort Lewis College with a music scholarship. She married a music teacher, Robert Ashley, who is also a blue grass banjo player. They have two grown children. Sandy and Bob recently retired from teaching careers in the Farmington, New Mexico system.

The Rico years were not well remembered by our mother. It wasn't only the hysterectomy that clouded her memory. From her free life, though it was a life of hardships, her life became one of being pregnant and tending to the cares of babies. She didn't escape the Little Yellow House like Dad did. Though there were neighbors, and caring friends, West Rico was a half-mile from the center of Rico.

Some years in Rico snow comes early, as early as September or October and the ground may not be seen again until April. I remember when my new little red wagon was covered with snow in the front yard in early winter and for me it was gone. Snow was so deep it didn't make a bump. When the snow melted in spring, I remember the little wagon had become very rusted. Our home had a very pitched metal roof, so snow slid off and piled up at the bottom of the eves. Many winters Dad had to shovel the snow away from windows to let natural light into the house.

And snow was so deep that we kids had to stay inside the house. Little legs just couldn't navigate the deep snow. Mother knew the need for Vitamin D that is normally built by the body in the skin when sunlight strikes the skin surface. Closed in at our home, cod liver oil was the source for the vitamin. Each morning it tasted so bad, and at our young ages we could not appreciate why we took the daily dose of that bad stuff from a spoon.

Looking back now, an important reason for Mom's discontent was the closeness of her Gage family. The Great Depression split the family in all directions to find work. Mom was closer to the family farm than her brothers and sisters, except for Fay. It was seventy-six miles from Rico to the Dove Creek farm. Though the farm and Rico were in the same county, come winters, and with three young children, she might as well have been two or three hundred miles from Dove Creek and family. Grandpa and Grandma Gage were still without a car and her mother was not well.

I contrast mother's life and feelings for Rico with those of Allie Baer, the town nurse. She came to Rico two years before Mom, spaced her children, and was integral to the welfare and success of the community. In an article written in a Cortez newspaper in the 1980s titled, "Allie Baer, from trading post to mining town—sixty years of change," she expresses how she loved life in Rico. She talks about the beautiful summer sunsets and the spirited community. But she also tells about her sadness when her children, at only fourteen, had to leave Rico to go to high school.

By 1942 the handwriting was on the wall. Dove Creek, the western incorporated town of Dolores County was booming with the farming of pinto beans. Its residents called Dove Creek, "The Pinto Bean Capital of the World." The population was increasing while the population of Rico was dwindling following World War II, yet it remained the county seat. And, of course, Rico did not have a high school. In Rico, Mom knew her time would come to say goodbye to her children for high school if the family remained there. With Mom's encouragement, Dad was looking to resign his elected position before Dove Creek became the new county seat. He resigned in 1942, but the County Commissioners persuaded him to wait for the next 1944 election. Dad would not let his name go on the ballot for the next election, and in March of 1944 he was hired as the Secretary and Treasurer of the Montezuma Valley Irrigation Company in Cortez. He began his new position on March 29, 1944, less than three weeks after the big early March storm that left Rico snowbound.

9

CORTEZ, THE HOUSING SHORTAGE, AND WORLD WAR II

On the tracks in front of the Rico Depot, the Galloping Goose is aimed toward Dolores. Mother and we three children boarded the Goose and would meet Dad at the Dolores Depot that day in early June of 1944. (Photograph from *The Rio Grand Story*, Volume 5, "Rico and the Mines")

Our dad lived the last of March, April, and into May of 1944 at the Cortez Hotel. As described earlier, Cortez was housing the Conscientious Objectors to World War II who were building the Jackson and Gulch Reservoir and the associated pipeline that would take water to the headquarters of Mesa Verde National Park. The few Cortez motels were full. There was no place for another family to live. A good Cortez friend of Dad's, Hank Thorpe, had just lost his wife. He had a teenage son and told Dad our family was welcome to live with him and his son, Gene.

The irrigation company that employed Dad sent its truck to Rico and our furniture was moved and put into storage in Cortez. Dad, took our little dog Bobby, and moved from the hotel to Hank's place. It was June and Mom with her three kids would ride the Galloping Goose from the Rico Depot and be picked up by Dad at the Dolores Depot.

We boarded the Goose. It was the last public transportation and freight transportation on the Rio Grande Southern Railroad before even the Goose for transportation ended a few years later. Though a sign on the door said, "No Pets," in its waning years, the Goose was very, very informal transportation, as we were soon to learn.

In a box, we had our momma cat and her kittens. Clickety click, down the rails we went—headed for Dolores. But the three cats did not know the rules and we were so hopeful that once on the way, the rules would not matter. The kittens began meowing. The driver looked at us and smiled. But a few miles further down the tracks we learned just how informal riding the Goose bus had become. A deer ran up onto the railroad grade and stopped. The driver stopped the Goose, took a rifle from beneath his seat and stepped out onto the tracks. It was June, and for sure not deer season. He may have only meant to scare the deer, because he shot and missed. He got back in the Goose without a comment. An hour or so later we met Dad at the Dolores Depot, cats and all.

The road from Dolores to Cortez was gravel until it met Highway 160, a mile east of Cortez. Cortez never had a railroad, not even a spur of a railroad. The announcement in the Cortez newspaper that Dad would be the new Secretary and Treasurer of the Montezuma Valley Irrigation ended with the statement that his family would join him in June, "...if they can find a home." The housing shortage caused by World War II was acute. Hank Thorpe owned a Cortez grocery store and his home was modest, not meant for three kids, Hank, Gene (his teenage son), Mom, and Dad. Hank was a kind friend of Dad's, who knew well the housing situation in Cortez. They lived in a small, three-bedroom home on Montezuma Avenue, a well-traveled road through residences in Cortez. Before we reached Hank's, Dad had brought Bobby, our medium sized dog, and moved in with Hank and Gene. Bobby was caught in a trapper's trap in Rico that left him with three legs for the ground and he carried a leg. Dad's love for dogs was beyond ordinary. He loved Bobby with four legs, but even more with three. He said Bobby knew math. He put down three and carried one. Car danger for Bobby was much greater on Montezuma Avenue in Cortez than in West Rico where the danger from cars was almost nil. One day Bobby was hit by a car and died. We were very saddened, but it made us realize the difficult situation we had accepted with Hank's goodwill. I don't remember the fate of our cats. My sister Beverly says they were taken to the Gage farm at Dove Creek.

Near the end of that 1944 summer, a room opened at the Navajo Court Motel that was located only two blocks from Dad's office at the irrigation company. We were glad to move to the single room unit, a cabin. It was in a row of cabins at the back end of the motel. I believe Conscientious Objectors occupied nearly all rooms of the motel. In the cabin we had to share common bathrooms and showers with these fellows. They were always very polite and seemed to understand the situation the war had caused. Everyone made sacrifices.

We three kids began attendance at the Cortez School that housed all twelve grades. Soon our family was able to rent a larger one-room unit at the front of the motel and it had a bathroom of its own. Next to the room, on the east side, was the Johnson Hospital where Barbara had been born and our Uncle Albia spent a long time following a highway construction accident.

The war in Europe with Germany, and the Axis countries and the Japanese in the Pacific, and even into the first post-war years, caused real shortages for civilians. Building materials were not available. The folks waited for any house to go on the market. A small house with an exterior of river stones was for sale. It was really out of desperation that Dad made a $100 deposit on the house and then he and Mom backed out and lost the $100. The house was just too small.

Another event to remember life in the one room motel room next door to the Johnson Hospital was when all three of us kids had chicken pox at the same time and couldn't go to school. Days were really long then for the five of us.

When I think of the Johnson Hospital, my Uncle Albia (Albie we called him) always comes to mind. He was Mom's older brother and we saw him rarely, but when we did, it was such a delight. His personality was just magnetic, always happy and so fun and easy to be around. He was married to Laura and they lived in Fontana, California.

When he was just a young man working on road construction near Cortez, Uncle Albie was severely injured from big road equipment. His back was broken, and he was taken to Johnson Hospital where he remained in traction for a long time. His injury handicapped him for life. He limped badly. The accident might have taken the smile off of most men's faces, but not Albie. We were so glad when he arrived to see us because he just lit the place up. He had gone through the Gage hardships and then the accident that he remembered with each step. And how he loved my mother. Like Mom, he just kept going. The worst of times didn't dim his spirit. Albie and Laura had one son, Alan, and he turned out to be just like his dad. He joined the California Highway Patrol. If I were to be stopped by a patrolman in California, let's hope it would be a patrolman as pleasant as Alan.

Johnson Hospital. (Photograph from *Cortez* by Vila Schwindt, Janet Weeth, and Dale Davidson)

But life in the one-room motel room was viewed as a sacrifice for the war and there were lighter times when the folks tried to make fun and enjoy recreating. Once on a picnic, Dad took a drink of lemonade and swallowed a seed. He left the table and immediately returned. He was looking for humor and had a leaf hanging from his mouth. He said the seed was already growing and coming up his throat. Mom didn't dampen the humor, but we kids, years six, seven, and eight, weren't so sure. Beverly and I saw the humor, but Barbara didn't think it was funny at all and was upset with Dad. Barbara always worried so easily.

Back in Rico, one time when we went into the courthouse, Dad led we three kids to the basement where the jail was. He had the keys. Rarely was the jail occupied since the majority of law-breakers in Dolores County who needed incarceration went to Cortez. It seemed to us that Dad was in charge of the courthouse. In fact, we referred to it as Daddy's Courthouse. Anyway, that day, with a smile on his face, he locked us in the jail, for about three minutes, and opened the door before Barbara would become worried.

On the route to school Barbara wouldn't cross the railroad tracks without Dad's hand. And she was very frightened if there was an engine near where we crossed to go up Depot Hill. She was an excellent student and an early reader. I remember how she could enter another world with a novel. In 1954, she was the salutatorian of her high school graduating class.

There were events and conditions of wartime I remember well in Cortez. I was in the second grade. There was no chocolate of any kind for sale. Chocolate candy bars were substituted with raisin bars and other sweetened grain alternatives for chocolate. Sugar was rationed, but it was gasoline for automobiles that folks use for driving that was missed most. Daily, my father picked up the mail sent to the irrigation company and he drove his own car. Mom and Dad needed to drive to Dove Creek because Grandma Gage was an invalid and Grandpa only had the tractor.

Harry Abilen was an elderly fellow who was caretaker of the irrigation company grounds. There were several buildings, including a large shop where flumes and head gates were built. Also, there was a large lumber storage shed. Harry Abilen drove an old International Pick-up a short distance to work and was rather recluse. He only had one eye. Harry always had gasoline stamps, was generous, and often gave Dad his extra stamps.

Most men of service age were in the war and the towns from 1941 until the end of the war were short of men of that age. There were no baseball games, and folks read the local newspaper's obituary section daily looking for the most recent deaths claimed by battles. Finally, Tuesday, May 8, 1945 was "Victory in Europe" (VE) Day, and it marked the end of Hitler's war. On that day in 1945, Great Britain, the United States and most all of Europe celebrated Victory in Europe. It ended six years of misery, suffering, unusual courage and endurance across the world. What a time of celebration it was. When word of the war's end reached Cortez, I don't know. Though I was only seven and would not be eight until June, May 8th, VE Day, was a day I remember well.

We lived in that single-room motel room on Main Street by Johnson Hospital and cars were going up and down the street (Highway 160) with horns honking. It was a time to feel really good and for many folks of Cortez, even better with plenty of alcohol. Dad never drank around the family, and only a beer now and then, like at the conclusion of Irrigation Board Meetings with the Directors. But sober or not, in our 1941 Chevy, the family aboard, we ventured onto the Main Street. What fun it was: horns honking, people walking the street laughing and yelling. It was a glorious evening. There were probably more drunk drivers in Cortez that evening and night than the small town had ever known or has known since.

Bang! Someone rear-ended us. Dad swore, which was rare for him with the family, and we returned to park the car in the overhang between rooms at our motel room. The Chevy was hardly damaged. Those cars in the forties had heavy chrome-plated bumpers. The minor collision didn't suppress our joy of the event, and with less fanfare, the celebration lived on for days.

Gradually, but not immediately, rationing of war essentials ended. The Navajo Court had a small convenience store that was on the corner with the motel on South Harrison and Main Street. The Jacksons who owned the motel where we lived, owned it. There was a second celebration after the war, and it was for us at Jackson's Store. Chocolate Hershey bars were back. Back, but not in abundance. Hershey bars at Jackson's were one per customer.

The war was over, but we still lived in the one-room unit of the motel. I guess Dad had shown his worth to the Montezuma Valley Irrigation Company. I believe he let the Board of Directors know he might have to leave the company and find a job where there was a place to live. It was at a meeting of the Board of Directors when the directors told Dad they were going to build him a house. A new one.

The building began immediately. In the motel, we were only a block from the site. The location for the new house was about a hundred feet west from the company house of Superintendent Bill Glen. We watched the new home come to be. The company Caterpillar dug a hole for a basement. Through that summer we watched the new house happen. But some house building supplies were not yet available, though it was nearly a year since the war ended. There wasn't wallboard. Hardwood for the floor was not available.

Bill Glen was a builder and though the main wooden structures the company built were head gates for water diversion and flumes, the company had a large mill where they sawed boards. So, Superintendent Glen used one inch by twelve-inch boards in place of wallboard. In that house, a picture, even heavy ones, could be hung anywhere. He took great pride in the house and as it went up and he often said to Dad, "It's the best built house in Cortez." It even had a second story with two upstairs bedrooms.

Superintendent Glen hired George Lions, a finishing carpenter who enjoyed a fine local reputation, to build drawers, kitchen cupboards, and anything else requested to make a house a home. Exactly when we moved in I don't recall, but what remains in our minds was how we expanded from life in the one room unit at Navajo Court. My sisters had a bedroom, I had one upstairs, and Mom and Dad's bedroom had the bed that came out of two years of storage. We even had a garden and a clothesline.

And with the location of our new home, the expanse of the irrigation company property around us, there was space available for athletic events that were high priority for me. I dug the pit and filled it with sawdust for high jumping and pole vaulting. We had a horseshoe-throwing site, croquet was played on the lawn, and there was space to play catch and hit a baseball. The sports locations at our place drew like-minded friends of mine from east Cortez.

It turns out these were not just ordinary child athletes from east Cortez that frequented the sports facilities provided close to our home on the Montezuma Valley Irrigation property. Jim Routt became a dentist. Darrell Higman became our high school quarterback, basketball guard and first baseman. In 1954 our football team for the season's opening game traveled 225 miles to play Grand Junction Central, the Tigers. Then it was the only high school in Grand Junction with a school population three times that of our school population of 500. Darrell ran back a punt and we won by seven. It was the only loss the Tigers took that year. They won the Division four state championship. Cortez was in Division 2. Darrell went on to be the fastest member of the University of Colorado Buffalo's baseball team. Most of his career was in school administration as the principal of high schools.

Besides a place to pitch horseshoes, play croquet, and the pole-vaulting pit, I had an indoor basketball court. It was the shed where the company's Caterpillar tractor was kept, but was rarely in its home. The superintendent allowed me to put up a backboard and basket. It had a concrete floor and room enough for a tightly played half-court game. Only a few close friends knew of the basketball court. One was Duane Woodard. We carried out one-on-one indoor games. He was fast and could dribble around me.

In Cortez, Duane lived with his father across the street, Highway 160, and he split time with his mother who lived in Casper, Wyoming. Duane was often at our place and I remember he played checkers with my Dad. Dad often remarked about how quick and competitive he was. He really liked to win and it would show when he beat Dad. Another admirable trait for his friendship with my father was his record keeping of baseball statistics — in his head.

Duane's Cortez teachers and all who spent time with him recognized his intellect. He graduated from Casper Natrona High School where he excelled as an athlete in football, wrestling and track. He joined the Marines after high school. Like for my sisters and me, money for college was in short supply. When he returned from the service he entered the University of Wyoming, received his BA degree in international studies and went on to the University of Oklahoma where he graduated with his J.D. degree from the College of Law.

But I never saw my friend again after Cortez, that is for a long time. But I knew of him. He served as the Attorney General of Colorado from 1983 to 1991. Then I was a professor at the University of Wyoming. The College of Arts and Sciences named Duane their Outstanding Alumnus in 2000 and in 2009 at the UW Homecoming Game with the University of New Mexico he was one of three alumni to receive the Distinguished Alumni Award.

As an alumnus Duane served UW in many ways and on the UW Foundation Board of Directors he learned from the College of Education magazine that I had retired but for many years I had been a professor of science education. He wrote me a letter. After so many years since he lived across Highway 160 in Cortez, our friendship was renewed.

Duane Woodard was bound for the Marines the very day he graduated from high school. he was with his platoon on a Luzon Island trail in the Philippines in 1957 when this photograph was taken. As Colorado Attorney General he was the Honored Guest and spoke at the Marine Corps Ball in Denver, 1985. (Photograph from Duane Woodard)

An event that brought a smile to my Dad's face with the war's ending, baseball was back. For every community it was like a celebration to form a baseball team. Soon there were more teams than existed prior to the war. Old rivalries were renewed. Ball fields were re-conditioned and new fields appeared. For Sunday afternoons, there was entertainment again. Games were social events. The townspeople looked forward to the weekend when cars would circle the field.

For big games, I remember cars two and three deep around the portion of the field near the grandstand. Mom and my sisters never got into baseball, but Dad's and my excitement was tolerated. We parked and Dad and I walked to the grandstand to get behind the batter's box. Beer was drunk openly in the stands and added to the game as extraneous entertainment.

Roy High was the catcher for the Cortez VFW team but if he wasn't playing with his team, he was in the bleachers with his friends and he was the center of attention with his wit. Two regular umpires were Jimmy Barrett, who, for a time was mayor of Cortez, and Rubidoux. Rube they called him. I probably never knew his first name. They were upper middle-aged men whom the town liked. It was fun at the games, though it was very serious competition. I remember once when Rubidoux was behind the bat umping a game, and when he called a pitch that the crowd didn't like, Roy High yelled out, "Poor ole Rube, Poor ole Rube. He hears a game going on, but he just can't find it!"

There were more post-war teams than I can remember, but some I remember in action were: Dove Creek, Cahone, Dolores, Goodman Point, Pleasant View, Durango, Rico, and Cortez had two teams. My team was the Cortez Veterans of Foreign Wars (the VFW) and it was during that immediate post-war time I learned the game and caught baseball fever. I remember many names of those VFW players: Floyd Ray (first base), Dean Hanson (short stop), Johnny Kuenstler (center field and homerun slugger), Roy High (catcher), Red Griffith (Burger Red was his nickname) third base. And for Dove Creek there was a very special player that later played with Cortez. He was Ernie Stevens. In World War II he was a driver for General Patton.

Before the war it was understood by southwestern Colorado baseball fans that they would someday see Ernie in the majors. Ernie Stevens was extremely fast and would play center field where he could cover a lot of territory. And he was such a batter. But in the war in Europe, Ernie was shot in his left arm and it became withered, almost entirely useless. He was right handed.

Ernie didn't let the handicap that kept him out of the pros keep him from his beloved sport. He caught the ball with a glove on his right hand, quickly put the glove with the ball under his withered left arm, pulled the ball out of the glove with his good hand and threw it, in a split second. The action became so rapid, some say, and as I would observe, it was so quick it was as though he had two functioning arms. And he batted with one arm very successfully. After Ernie came to Cortez, he played for Cortez and became a little league coach. He was my coach. What a patient and complete coach he was, especially a batting coach. We young players learned how, with one arm, he hit the ball more often than most of the two-armed batters.

Some of the games I remember well, but probably not like Dad. But baseball, locally and nationally, was our common language and we shared that interest for his entire life. Of course, he was in his late forties and became fifty in those post-war years and was only a fan and observer. But he was my best fan when I played for the little league teams and caught two years in high school and pitched my senior year. But never did I "hit the ball" like Dad.

In the summer of 1947, we were living in the new home that was built for us. I had turned 11 and the Cortez VFW team would be playing the Rico Miners in July. Dad was anxious for the game. Finally, it was that Sunday, the day of the game. In our 41 Chevy we were headed up the dusty Dolores River road to watch that very memorable Rico versus Cortez game. This book of memories has come full circle.

POSTSCRIPT

I can picture Mom fastening her snow boots and beginning the two-mile walk in deep snow to meet children who were hungry and only would have a boiled ear of corn for lunch. I knew of her courage and determination at forty-five to get in the car headed to Fort Lewis College with boys who were recent high school graduates. I see her take her place in a classroom surrounded by students who were young enough to be her children. And in California, her younger sister was doing much the same to make her family's welfare better. When all the potatoes froze and the crop that was to be sold and sustain the family through the winter didn't happen, it was through love and sharing that saved them.

There was courage on both sides of my family. It was desperation, and it took courage for Grandfather and Grandmother Keown to strike out for Dove Creek into a land of unknown circumstances, grub out the sagebrush, and begin farming a homestead.

Dad stepped in to take leadership of the family when he was only nineteen. No one was making it by farming, and with courage he went to work on the railroad, mine, or in the mills. But especially, it took courage to face the possibility of failure in the county election, to assume a white-collar position (wearing a tie to work), knowing his education had been only ten grades in Blanca. What would be expected of him, and who would help him if he didn't know the answers to challenging questions that went with managing the county's money?

The depression was setting in and his job was to get the county's employees paid when citizens couldn't pay their taxes. He survived the challenges and became very successful at his line of work. It changed his life, but he did not do it alone. None of us survive alone. Our dad found Rowena Snyder, the county clerk, to help him and was able to communicate and learn. Communication is the distinguishing characteristic of our species and it was Dad's special gift, even beyond "hitting the ball." He could talk to people.

Let's look back at 100 plus years of change. From Dad's childhood friend calling him from the tent, "Herald, let's go see the atom-biele," to spacecrafts, my folks' time saw so much change. And with great anticipation, our parents and the world watched on July 20, 1969 when men walked on the moon.

They went through the 1918 Influenza, two World Wars, the Korean Conflict and Vietnam. The Kennedy brothers were assassinated and there was so much social change. The families experienced the Prohibition, the Great Depression, radios became common, and so did TVs. I remember our first telephone when we moved into the home that the irrigation company built for us.

Children are born totally dependent on their parents, especially their mother; more dependent than most species. But at first they have an empty mind. A developing mind is like the continuous assemblage of a very complex program for a computer. It becomes their field of reference. Parents are input with their behaviors, their language and its complexity and diversity. Friends add to the field of reference, religious beliefs are learned; rituals and the child's exchange with the natural and manmade world are input to the child's brain program. The field of reference is never static. That program becomes the mind, and for some children it may change but little from the likes of their parents as they face the changing world. However, the education experience, whether public or private, is (or should be), the avenue to a larger and diverse field of reference.

My parents were caring and loving, uncommonly good examples as parents. On a trip home from my professorship position in Science Education at the University of Wyoming, the subject of the Old Testament and beliefs it teaches became the topic at a dinner meal. I realized how my parents and my "fields of reference" had grown apart. The story of Noah's Ark came up and I began to talk about inconsistencies with the reality of putting all of Earth's species onto a 300 foot boat and floating the seas for forty days. The Biblical story has so many violations of the laws of nature that it isn't taken literally by most men and women of our time. The story is in such conflict with ecological evidence. Some animals have never been housed successfully, not even in the most modern zoos. How much hay, or any other elephant food, would two elephants eat in forty days? How about the storage of the great varieties of food necessary, and water? How did Noah get those two muskoxen from the frozen arctic to the warm Middle East? And two tapirs from South America across the Atlantic Ocean? Hummingbirds live on the edge of survival and can starve to death in three to five hours. And very problematic were the human parasites.

In Genesis, God says "every living substance was to be destroyed" by the flood. After the folks had passed away I read the classic article by Robert A. Moore, "The Impossible Voyage of Noah's Ark," in the journal, *Creation/Evolution*. It was a lengthy discussion about the many impossibilities of Noah's voyage. He concludes his article with an amusing fact about parasites. Nearly all species carry parasites. Humans carry an assortment that are obligate parasites, meaning they will not live on any species but us. Some of these are a species of tapeworm, the intestinal worm Ascaris lumbricoides, the hookworm, the pinworm, three species of lice, and five species of venereal disease.

Noah and his family of eight must have carried these aboard. As the author Moore writes, "The unfortunate souls were afflicted with enough disease and discomfort to support a hospital." My evidence rattled on and Mom turned to Dad and said, "We believe in Noah's Ark."

My biological education changed my field of reference. Most factors in our fields of references remain unchanged and useful; while we delete ideas, we add understanding that changes how we interpret the world. This is what education should be.

Let me continue to wrap up this ending unit of the book by looking at events Mom and Dad lived to see, and some they didn't live to see. Some events gave them delight, and some they may have been fortunate to escape.

Dad, baseball lover that he was, didn't see the Colorado Rockies come into the major leagues in 1991. He would have enjoyed seeing them in the World Series in 1997, even though they lost to the Boston Red Sox in four games.

Mom wanted to see the Bible Lands, the birthplace of Jesus and places the Bible describes. To travel to Grand Junction, two hundred plus miles from Cortez, was a long adventure for Dad. Long travel experiences were nervously anticipated and unpleasant.

Our astronauts live in space, men and women both in the capsule. After the long lapse of landing on the moon, plans are aloft to land on Mars. I won't see that one either. It will be another fete some of us believe should be preceded by our international effort to make peace and cease warring. The folks would be with me on this. Wars unjustly take lives, but they also ravage habitats of species. They take enormous quantities of natural resources — some vital to our modern technology.

And there were events that garnered less publicity that have immeasurably changed our species' future. The folks' fields of reference were without preparation for these significance events. And such was the field of reference for most citizens. They were less understood than the first footprints on the moon.

James Watson, Francis Crick, with the x-ray of crystallographer Rosalind Franklin, transformed biology with their 1953 discovery of the molecular structure of deoxyribonucleic acid: DNA — the building code molecule for all life. Resultant of the DNA discovery, the genetic code for building human insulin is plugged into bacteria and that pioneer form of life makes insulin for diabetics. And the effort by geneticists and associated biologists worldwide brought us the identification of the genes that make up the human genetic code, our genome. It is the code the fertilized egg (the zygote) uses to form us, our species, you and me. We know today why there is the great diversity of life. The diversity of life occurs because of seemingly minor differences in the arrangement of the few base chemicals that line up to form the double helix of DNA. The specific lineup of the bases caused *Tyrannosaurus rex.*

And at that dinner meal with the folks when I went nowhere with science versus Noah's Ark, I didn't venture into organic evolution. But a word must be said about evolution in this wrap-up because so few, even the college graduates who take the required introductory biology class, as Mom did, don't relate themselves with the millions of species whose variation in DNA came down the same path that makes us their kin.

We are so biologically connected, yet, for most of our time we've seen our species apart. I have been to the bottom of the Grand Canyon four times; three of those hikes were with my students. To walk to the bottom of the canyon is to pass through the rock record of Earth's history. Earth isn't 6,000 years old as Creationists would have us believe. Science says it is 4.6 billion years old. If the history of Earth's 4.6 billion year history had been filmed and the film condensed to a one-year movie, 365 days, 6,000 years would occupy the last 21 seconds of the film. Ourselves and Earth's millions of species are at the zenith of this creation and that knowledge should give us a view unlike our ancestors—a great desire to preserve.

Science education is about bridging the concrete minds of children, and I must add many adults, to the abstract ideas of science. The age of the Earth links Darwin and Wallace's great discovery of the 19th century, and Watson, Crick and Franklin's discovery, with the time element necessary for the great diversity of Earth's life to evolve. I wish my folks might have had the opportunity to realize the meaning of the great discoveries of these scientists and how knowing the great age of Earth unifies the relationship of the millions of species on Earth that have evolved.

And how do we treat that diversity? Because of the great age of the Earth, our time now should be the pinnacle in number of species. Yet we live in a human-caused era of extinction. Stephen Gould, the late, great paleontologist said that bacteria, with a relatively simple genome, might still dominate this planet. Even if our species' consumption, pollution, and abuse of the biosphere take out the higher species, bacteria will live on. They get the last bite of everything. That perishing thought takes us from this life science essay to the final topics of this postscript, more changes my folks saw, or didn't see.

President Richard Nixon signed the Environmental Protection Act, The Endangered Species Act, The Clean Water Act, and the Clean Air Act in the early seventies. The folks would have said Hooray! They saw the changes these laws brought. The thousands of mine dumps in Colorado and toxic sites in all states would begin to be cleaned up, ones that nineteenth and twentieth century mine and mill operations walked away from. It has cost billions to reclaim the sites but worth every nickel. The toxic ponds of the Rico Argentine Mining Company in Rico poisoned the Dolores River all the way to Dolores. The leaking ponds were pictured in the National Geographic. Sites are classified for their toxicity and danger. The worst made the list of the Toxic 500. The whole town of Leadville, Colorado was on the list and on the edge of Laramie, Wyoming, where I live, remnants of a large pond where railroad ties were floated in creosote made the Toxic 500.

Our parents didn't live to see so many humans become a virtual species. With cell phones we don't look at each other when we communicate, and anyone can go online and pontificate to the world theories and news they know nothing about. There is an addiction that has replaced reality, 60 Minutes reporter, Anderson Cooper, relates. It especially affects teens. For many, a real anxiety develops when they are away from their cell phones. The phone prevents the child from being "present" in this life. Our lives in the past were close to nature, or at least to the nature of rural life. Mom and Dad missed most of this virtual communication. For her teaching, Mom would loved to have read, *Last Child in the Woods* by Richard Louv.

Neither Mom nor Dad were naturalists, but they encouraged preservation of wildlife and wildflower species. Mom took a wildflowers workshop, and could name and knew about several species of wildflowers. They were so proud of my accomplishments at environmental education in public education in Utah and at the University of Wyoming. I wish they could have been in Portland in the fall of 2009. As reported locally, "Dr. Duane Keown, retired University of Wyoming Professor of Science Education, was honored at the Annual Conference of the North American Association for Environmental Education in Portland, Oregon. He received the distinguished Outstanding Service to Environmental Education by an Individual Award for 2009." The NAAEE (North American Association for Environment Education) has thousands of members in fifty-five nations. Also, my parents would like to have been at an honorary gathering November 8, 2019 in Laramie when I received the lifetime service award for Contribution to Biodiversity Conservation from the Biodiversity Institute at the University of Wyoming.

Dad loved the small towns where he knew everyone. In the cities, he would tighten his grip on the steering wheel, tense up and wish he had stayed home. He experienced how our nation had grown in population in his time and probably realized how it affected community behavior. Freedom is affected.

In 1900, when Dad was four years old, the U.S. population was 76.2 million. When he was 44, the population was 132 million and in 1981 when Mom died, it was 229.5 million. In 2021 the U.S population will be more than 330 million. In Dad's lifetime the U.S. population increased more than three times.

Many factors affect freedom of people, but population density is always a factor. New Jersey has the greatest population density in the U.S. today at 1,211 persons per square mile. My home state of Wyoming is sparsely populated with six persons per square mile but outdone by Alaska with only 1.2 persons per square mile. My parents liked the wide-open spaces of Wyoming, but once they visited in February, and as they were leaving, the wind slammed the storm door shut behind them. When they stepped into the icy cold, Mom turned to me and said, "You aren't going to live here long, are you?" That was forty-five years ago.

As I write this postscript my wife and I are most days in hibernation and carry out the behaviors that go with avoiding the COVID-19 virus. The U.S. death toll caused by the disease reached 509,596 yesterday and the slope on the deaths curve will continue upward until the population realizes we all must join in prevention behaviors and take a vaccine. When we turn on the news tonight, what will the new toll be?

I really wish my parents could have known my wife, Joy. I was divorced from my first wife in 1982 and for twenty years after I was single. On July 17, 2002 I married Joy and we both retired from our career positions. She was a high school biological sciences teacher in Torrington, Wyoming and for nearly thirty years. I was a Science Education Professor at the University of Wyoming.

As Vice President under Dwight Eisenhower, Dad liked Nixon and when he became president our father was a very loyal supporter. Then came the Watergate scandal. Dad believed Nixon could do no wrong. At the time I was leading environmental education at Monticello High School and bringing my parents into the movement. I admired Nixon when he signed laws that would sustain and improve our environment. When Watergate became Nixon's scandal, Dad wrote Nixon a letter of support. Nixon may have sent thousands of thank you letters to his supporters. Dad took his letter, framed it, and hung it on the wall. But when the tapes came out that made Nixon the century's most famous liar, even before Senate Republican loyalist like Barry Goldwater turned on him, Dad took Nixon's framed letter from the wall like it was burning a hole. Dad's action was in line with his devotion to honesty.

ACKNOWLEDGMENTS

Joy, my wife, takes on my many projects like they were her own and makes them a partnership, and is always the first reader of what I write, or packing our packs for a long wilderness hike and adventure. She looks for birds and plants. She is a naturalist. I met her in her employment as Ranger Naturalist in Yellowstone.

It is expected, maybe not routine, that we see our parents as special people, not because they were our originators, but for the many values, behaviors and their traits we observe and learn in growing with them. My sisters and I were the lucky ones to have such idyllic parents for me to write about. My deceased sister Barbara would thank me for my effort to spread the word about Dad and Mom and relate the times and experiences of their lives. But especially, I am grateful for my younger sister Beverly (Keown) Donovan, only a year younger, who lives in California and has talked the contents of this book with me so many times. And since my folks passing, she has been the keeper of the "old trunk" that surprised us when we discovered so much history of the lives and times gone by of our parents. With her and my wife's encouragement, I tell of our family's interesting and dauntless histories.

Next comes Glen Baer, a personal friend for 77 years, since we entered the first grade at Rico School in 1943. I left Rico when the family moved down river to Cortez in 1944. Glen came to Cortez in 1951 for the ninth grade. Rico has never had a high school. When he learned of this project he contributed with enthusiasm. And he knows Rico much better than I. He and his siblings spend time in the old town and still own the home of their departed parents. It was a joy to write about his mother, a nurse and known locally as the Mother Teresa of Rico.

Duane Woodard has been a friend for almost as long as Glen. In Cortez he lived across Highway 160 from me and we played sports together. As a retired Attorney General for Colorado (1983–1991), a member of the University of Wyoming Foundation Board, and graduate of UW, he renewed his friendship with me when he learned I retired from his university. We rehash our histories and Cortez times.

It was a labor of love to search out the regions where our parent's lives happened, to see the sites of their experiences. In the San Luis Valley of southern Colorado, I thank the local historian Shannon Hard who contributed Blanca, Colorado history and photographs. I wouldn't leave out Eric Carpio and Joe Gallegos at the Fort Garland History and Culture Museum and pictures they contributed. They led me to the resource Shannon Hard was.

In Dove Creek the County Treasurer, Janie Stiasny, made my wife and I aware of the local historian, Audrey Garchar. She helped us find the not often traveled roads that led to the early twentieth century homesteads of the Keowns near Dove Creek and first Colorado home of Gages at Bug Point.

Molly Warren compiled a history of Montezuma and Dolores County schools with her *Montezuma Trails of Time*. It is with sites, persons and photographs. It was used extensively to capture my mom's one room school teaching days. And the authors of *Cortez,* Vila Schwindt, Janet Weeth and Dale Davidson, allowed me to use photos from their Cortez history book.

And there were the Gage and Keown cousins. Their memories of the family histories were with great variance but certainly with interest. Norman Gage, son of my mother's youngest brother Fay, was an important and enthusiastic contributor to Gage history.

And Wayne Cook in Chico, California has an exceptional zeal for Gage history. Carol (Cook) Carr knew of her mother Edith (Gage) Cook's love of farming and her drive to see her children educated.

Serendipitous records of our parents family lives came without planning, like the old newspaper accounts of the murder of Alfred Rittenhouse by Albert McGee in 1931. Granddad Gage, the County Sheriff, made the arrest and handcuffed McGee to his own bed the night before the trip to the Cortez jail. Sally Jo Leitner, a researcher at the Cortez Library, found articles dating to early 1930s.

www.ingramcontent.com/pod-product-compliance
Lightning Source LLC
Chambersburg PA
CBHW070331090426
42733CB00012B/2445